GLOBE

The
AUCKLAND

GRAEME LAY

GLOBETROTTER™

Second edition published in 2007
by New Holland Publishers Ltd
London • Cape Town • Sydney • Auckland
First published in 2004
10 9 8 7 6 5 4 3 2 1
website: www.newhollandpublishers.com

Garfield House, 86 Edgware Road
London W2 2EA United Kingdom

80 McKenzie Street
Cape Town 8001, South Africa

14 Aquatic Drive
Frenchs Forest, NSW 2086, Australia

218 Lake Road
Northcote, Auckland, New Zealand

Distributed in the USA by
The Globe Pequot Press, Connecticut

Copyright © 2007 in text: Graeme Lay
Copyright © 2007 in maps: Globetrotter
Travel Maps
Copyright © 2007 in photographs:
Individual photographers as credited (right)
Copyright © 2007 New Holland Publishers
(UK) Ltd

All rights reserved. No part of this publication
may be reproduced, stored in a retrieval system
or transmitted, in any form or by any means,
electronic, mechanical, photocopying, recording
or otherwise, without the prior written permission of the publishers and copyright holders.

ISBN 978 1 84537 808 0

Although every effort has been made to ensure
that this guide is up to date and current at time of
going to print, the Publisher accepts no responsibility or liability for any loss, injury or inconvenience
incurred by readers or travellers using this guide.

Publishing Manager: Thea Grobbelaar
DTP Cartographic Manager: Genené Hart
Editors: Carla Zietsman, Melany McCallum
Designers: Nicole Bannister, Lellyn Creamer
Cartographers: Tanja Spinola, Lucian Packies

Reproduction by Hirt & Carter (Pty) Ltd,
Cape Town

Printed and bound by Times Offset (M) Sdn. Bhd.,
Malaysia

Photographic Credits:

Alexander Turnbull Library: page 8;
Gerald Cubitt: pages 23, 36, 81;
Don Donovan: page 39;
Hutchison Image Library/Robert Francis: pages 21, 84;
Hutchison Image Library/Andrew Sole: page 46;
jonanoldimages.com/Doug Pearson: pages 6, 37;
Caroline Jones: pages 14, 72;
Graeme Lay: page 77;
Life File Images/Paul Miles: page 80;
Bob McCree: title page, pages 7, 17, 19, 22, 24, 25, 26, 28, 29, 30, 31, 32, 33, 34, 35, 38, 41, 46, 48, 50, 54, 60, 61, 66, 68, 70, 73, 75, 78, 79, 83;
Photo Access/Sime: cover;
Pictures Colour Library: pages 13, 27, 53;
Neil Setchfield: pages 11, 15, 16, 18, 20;
Robin Smith: page 82;
Jeroen Snijders: pages 12, 42, 45, 65;
Travel Ink/Nigel McCarthy: page 40.

Front Cover: *A view of Auckland's skyline from the marina.*
Title Page: *The Auckland Harbour Bridge connects the two shores of the Waitemata Harbour.*

CONTENTS

Using This Book	4
Overview	6
The Land	7
History in Brief	8
Government & Economy	11
The People	12
The Arts	13
Highlights	14
The Auckland Museum	14
The Viaduct Harbour	15
The Sky Tower	16
Kelly Tarlton's Antarctic Encounter and Underwater World	17
Devonport by Ferry	18
The West Coast Beaches	19
The New Zealand National Maritime Museum	20
Albert Park	21
The Museum of Transport and Technology (MOTAT)	22
Auckland Zoo	23
The Waitakere Ranges	24
Auckland's Regional Parks	25
Long Bay Regional Park	26
The Waitemata Waterfront	27
Central City Library	28
Cornwall Park	29
Mount Eden	30
Parnell Road	31
Ponsonby	32
Titirangi	33
Sightseeing	34
The North Shore	34
East Coast Bays	34
Lake Pupuke	35
The Hauraki Gulf and its Islands	36
Rangitoto Island	37
Historic Buildings	38
Religious Buildings	39
Art Galleries	39
Activities	41
Sport and Recreation	41
Fun for Children	43
City Walks	45
Organized Tours	48
Shopping	50
Shops	50
Markets	52
Accommodation	54
Where to Stay	54
Hotels	55
Eating Out	60
What to Eat	60
Where to Eat	61
What to Drink	65
Wineries	67
Where to Drink	68
Entertainment	70
Nightlife	70
Theatres	72
Cinemas	73
Events	74
Festivals	75
Excursions	78
Wenderholm Regional Park	78
Matakana to Tawharanui	79
Waiheke	80
Tiritiri Matangi	81
Great Barrier	82
Kawau	83
Travel Tips	84
Index of Sights	92
General Index	93

USING THIS BOOK

MAKE THE MOST OF YOUR GUIDE

Reading these two pages will help you to get the most out of your guide and save you time when using it. Sites discussed in the text are cross-referenced with the cover maps – for example, the reference 'Map A–C3' refers to the Auckland City Map (Map A), column C, row 3. Use the Map Plan below to quickly locate the map you need.

MAP PLAN

Outside Back Cover   Outside Front Cover

Inside Front Cover   Inside Back Cover

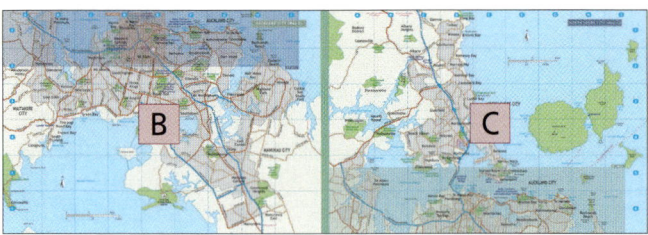

THE BIGGER PICTURE

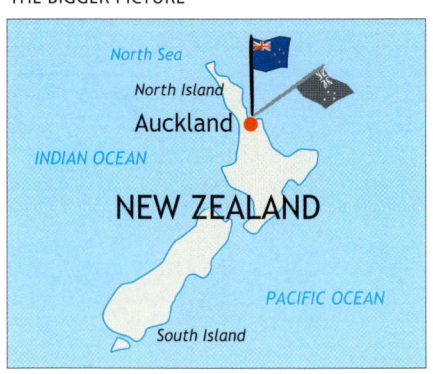

Key to the Map Plan

A – Auckland City Centre
B – Auckland City
C – North Shore City
D – Excursions from Auckland

Using this Book

Key to Symbols

- ✉ — address
- ☎ — telephone
- 📠 — fax
- 💻 — website
- 🖱 — e-mail address
- 🕒 — opening times
- 🚌 — tour
- 💰 — entry fee
- 🍽 — restaurants nearby
- **M** — nearest metro station

Map Legend

motorway	━━━	main road	Albert
national road	━━━	other road	Lorne
main road	━━━	shopping centre	Three Lamps Centre ⓢ
minor road	━━━	one-way street	↘
railway	━━━	built-up area	▫
river	Wainui	hotel	Ⓗ SEBEL
route number	①	building of interest	Auckland University
city	AUCKLAND	library	📖
large village	◉ Orewa	post office	✉
village	○ Wainui	parking area	🅿
peak	Tararu ▲ 695 m	tourist information	ⓘ
area name	Parnell	place of worship	△ Auckland Hebrew
airport	✈	police station	●
		bus terminus	🚌
place of interest	★ Parnell Rose Gardens	hospital	✚
		park & garden	Newmarket Park

Keep us Current

Travel information is apt to change, which is why we regularly update our guides. We'd be most grateful to receive feedback from you if you've noted something we should include in our updates. If you have any new information, please share it with us by writing to the Publishing Manager, Globetrotter, at the office nearest to you (addresses on the imprint page of this guide). The most significant contribution to each new edition will be rewarded with a free copy of the updated guide.

OVERVIEW

Above: *The Westhaven Marina and Sky Tower (background, right).*

Climate
Auckland's maritime setting means that it experiences no extremes of climate. February has the highest average, 24°C (75°F), and June–August the coolest (15°C, 59°F), wettest conditions. Early summer is often humid, and in both spring and summer there can be spectacular subtropical deluges. Annual rainfall is 1200mm (47in) and there are an average of 245 days of sunshine per year. There are few windless days at any time of the year, but frosts are rare. Summer and autumn offer the best weather. February to May are settled and warm, ideal for walking, swimming, boating and barbecuing – the activities preferred by most Aucklanders.

AUCKLAND
Sprawling, dynamic and cosmopolitan, Auckland with its 1.3 million people is New Zealand's largest and most magnetic city. Except for a brief period in the 1870s, when it was temporarily overtaken by Dunedin, Auckland has held its position as New Zealand's primary urban centre since its beginnings in the 1840s. Shamelessly commercial since its inception, Auckland continues to draw immigrants from all parts of New Zealand, as well as from a myriad of other countries.

Spreading across a small (only about 20 by 10km [12 by 6 miles]) isthmus which occupies the North Island's narrowest point, Auckland is blessed with two fine harbours. The **Waitemata** on its eastern side is an inlet of the **Pacific Ocean**; the **Manukau** to the west opens to the **Tasman Sea**. Aucklanders' love of the sea and the huge number of yachts in their harbours makes the city's sobriquet, 'The City of Sails', singularly apt.

The **Tamaki Isthmus**, studded with extinct volcanic cones, connects these two sheltered expanses of sea, a land bridge which has attracted human occupation – Polynesian and European – for hundreds of years.

New Zealand's largest manufacturing centre, the city has now spread north and south of the isthmus, and draws tens of thousands of immigrants each year, adding more and more human layers to its unique geographical character. An international survey in 2003 ranked Auckland the fifth best city in the world (highest ranked city in the Southern Hemisphere) for its 'quality of life'.

THE LAND

The Land
Climate

Auckland experiences a temperate maritime climate of long warm summers and moist cool winters. Spring is a short and sharp season, followed by a long summer which gradually drifts into an autumn that lasts for several months. Swimming and boating, the favourite recreational pursuits of Aucklanders, are possible from November through to May, allowing locals and visitors to savour the beauty of the city's long coastline and two sheltered harbours.

Environment

Almost totally surrounded by the two seas which lap at its front and back doorsteps, Auckland is also blessed with several manmade and natural parks. Adjoining the central city is tranquil **Albert Park**, a short drive away is the undulating green expanse of the **Domain**, and to the west of the city are the magnificent **Waitakere Ranges**, a broad volcanic wall covered in native forest and laced with walking tracks. Scattered across the isthmus are several volcanic cones whose slopes are grassy reserves and from whose summits there are panoramic views of the city and its harbours. In the nearby **Hauraki Gulf**, off the east coast of Auckland, are a number of beautiful islands (many of which are reserves) that can be visited by boat or ferry. The brooding presence of the largest and newest volcanic island, **Rangitoto**, guards the city's harbour entrance like a green giant.

> **The Naming of Auckland**
>
> In 1840 the first European governor of the new British colony, William Hobson, named New Zealand's first capital 'Auckland', after his naval commander and patron, the First Earl of Auckland. The city's European place names are redolent of its British imperial upbringing e.g. Queen Street, Queens Wharf, Albert Street, Mount Victoria, Victoria Street, Khyber Pass Road.

Below: *Hang-gliding from North Head, Devonport, with Rangitoto Island in the background.*

OVERVIEW

Land Reclamation
Although Auckland relinquished its capital status to more centrally located Wellington in 1865, the town continued to grow rapidly. The expansion of commercial activity around the Waitemata waterfront, the focus of the shipping trade, led to extensive reclamation of the foreshore from the 1860s onwards. The reclaimed land comprised mainly soil and rock hewn from the removal of Britomart and Smales Points, headlands that faced the shore. This permitted the town to extend its commercial area, and meant that all the buildings on the level land between the junction of Shortland and Queen Streets and the harbour are built on land reclaimed from the sea in the latter half of the 19th century.

History in Brief

The first Aucklanders were migrants from eastern Polynesia who had travelled to the place they called **Aotearoa** ('Land of the Long White Cloud') in canoes, and then dispersed throughout the land. However, the exact time of their arrival is indeterminable, as urban growth has obliterated most of the sites which may have yielded definite prehistoric evidence. Settlement of the central isthmus and gulf islands probably began between the 13th and 14th centuries AD.

Maori soon established themselves on the isthmus, finding its wasp-waist topography ideal for hauling canoes from one coast of the North Island to the other. At **Otahuhu**, (the Tamaki isthmus's narrowest point), the North Island is only 1km (0.6 miles) wide, permitting Maori to haul their vessels overland from the Pacific Ocean to the Tasman Sea, thereby eliminating a 1000km (620-mile) journey around North Cape. The Maori called the portage at Otahuhu *Te Towaka*, 'The Dragging Place of Canoes'.

Maori also prized the Tamaki isthmus for its estuaries and harbours, which were rich

in seafood, its fertile volcanic soils, its subtropical forests, which had plentiful edible berries, fern-root and birds, and its volcanic cones, which made ideal *pa* (Maori settlement) sites. Feuding between rival tribes over the isthmus was endemic, however, and by the time the first European arrivals saw Tamaki-makaurau, the area had been laid

8

History in Brief

waste by intertribal fighting and was almost devoid of people. Earlier, the isthmus had been home to the **Wai-o hua** people, until the mid-18th century, when they were attacked and defeated by **Ngati Whatua**. In the 1820s the **Nga Puhi** invaded and forced the Ngati Whatua into exile. They returned, however, in the late 1830s and even today are accorded *tangata whenua* status, which means they are the traditional guardians of the land and sea around the isthmus.

The English seafarer **James Cook** did not discover the Waitemata Harbour on his epic 1769 voyage around New Zealand. The distinction of being the first European to enter Auckland's main harbour went to Sydney-based English missionary **Samuel Marsden**, who in 1820 explored the upper reaches of the Waitemata. After New Zealand became an official colony of Britain with the signing of the Treaty of Waitangi in the Bay of Islands on 6 February 1840, the first governor, **William Hobson RN** had the responsibility of selecting a site for a new capital.

Hobson chose a landing site on the southern shore of the Waitemata Harbour. The appeals of this site were the two harbours and proximity to fertile land. Hobson began negotiations to buy land from the Ngati Whatua chiefs. In October 1840, a 1214ha (3000-acre) wedge of land was purchased from Ngati Whatua for 'five pounds of money' and sundry goods, including clothing, tobacco and pipes, kitchen utensils and hatchets. A ship, *Anna Watson,* brought the first settlers from Russell in the Bay of Islands, which had been the first sizeable European settlement in New Zealand. The base of the land purchased by Hobson was

---

The Auckland Harbour Bridge
In the 19th and 20th centuries, Auckland's city fathers dreamed of a bridge that would connect the southern and northern shores of **Waitemata Harbour**. This became a reality in 1959, when a four-lane bridge from **Point Erin** on the city side to **Northcote Point** on the North Shore was opened. It had taken four years to build, was 1.02km (0.6 miles) long, contained 6000 tons of steel and was the last lattice girder bridge to be built in the world.

In its first year some 13,000 vehicles used it per day. Getting from the North Shore to the city was now easy, so the North Shore suburbs expanded rapidly. By 1969 an average of 41,000 vehicles per day were using it and two extra lanes were added on either side. Today, over 150,000 vehicles a day use the bridge. For a guided climb along the arch of the bridge, contact **Auckland Bridge Climb**,
☎ 0800 462 5462
💻 www.auckland bridgeclimb.co.nz
Bungy jumps are also possible.

Opposite: *Captain William Hobson RN, first Governor of New Zealand.*

OVERVIEW

Auckland's Fathers
Among Auckland's many mayors, two in particular stand out:
John Logan Campbell (1817–1912), a Scot, was one of the first European settlers in Auckland. A successful farmer, merchant, author (*Poenamo* 1881) and philanthropist, he donated his parkland, **One Tree Hill**, to the city. One of his houses, **Acacia Cottage**, Auckland's oldest house (built in 1840), is in the park and a statue of 'the father of Auckland', as he was known, stands at the gate of the reserve. His grave is on the hill's summit. (*See* page 29.)

Sir Dove Meyer Robinson (1901–89) was Auckland's longest-serving mayor. Elected twice, he held office from 1959–65 and from 1968–80. A colourful individual, civic visionary and environmentalist, his main contribution to the city was the implementation of a proper sewerage treatment scheme rather than the plan to discharge sewage into the Waitemata Harbour. His statue is on the Queen Street side of Aotea Square, and the gardens in Gladstone Road, Parnell, are called Dove Meyer Robinson Park.

Opposite: *Queen Street is Auckland city's main commercial thoroughfare.*

the southern shore of the Waitemata Harbour, its apex the highest volcanic cone, **Maungawhau** (Mount Eden). Today this land comprises by far the most valuable area of real estate in New Zealand.

19th-century History

In 1840 a concentric town plan was laid out on paper by the Government's Surveyor General, **Felton Mathew**. This was, however, largely ignored in favour of development at Hobson's main landing site, Commercial Bay, and the Ligar Creek (later Ligar Canal), which followed the route of present-day Queen Street. In 1842 the ships *Jane Gifford* and *Duchess of Argyle* brought 550 settlers, mainly from Scotland, to their new home. During the 1840s and '50s, the new town flourished through government business, land speculation, farming and trade. The waterfront was centred on **Commercial Bay** – a small inlet between Britomart Point and Smales Point. An administrative and military centre and trading port, Auckland also became a centre for the woodworking and boat-building industries that drew on the kauri forests of the town's hinterland.

Later the suburbs spread out from the central city to **Parnell** and **Remuera** (east), **Herne Bay** and **Ponsonby** (west) and **Mount Eden** (south). An extensive tram system connected these suburbs with Queen Street, and a ferry service across the Waitemata connected **Devonport** with the centre. In the 1870s and '80s, a surge in immigration increased the population from 7000 in 1861 to 33,000 in 1891. By 1896 the population of the Auckland Metropolitan area was 51,000; by 1911 it had reached 103,000.

GOVERNMENT AND ECONOMY

The 20th Century

Throughout the 20th century Auckland remained New Zealand's largest city. The Waitemata was the country's largest port for exports and imports, suburbs spread across the Tamaki isthmus and a large part of the city was devoted to manufacturing. Growth continued to accelerate – the fastest growth being from the late 1940s onwards. In 1945 the city had fewer people than Wellington and Christchurch combined, but by 1975 Auckland had as many people (743,000) as the next biggest three cities combined. By the mid-1970s Auckland had a quarter of New Zealand's population, a third of whom were employed in manufacturing. Plentiful jobs, a congenial climate and good lifestyle drew more migrants to Auckland from other parts of New Zealand and from overseas.

Government and Economy

The city of Auckland is now home to over 1.3 million people, or one out of every four New Zealanders. It extends from **Torbay** in the north to **Papakura** in the south, and from the **Waitakere Ranges** in the west to **Waiheke Island** in the east. For administrative purposes, Auckland is four cities in one. These separately administered cities are **North Shore** (north), **Waitakere** (west), **Auckland City** (central isthmus, including the islands of the Hauraki Gulf) and **Manukau City** (south). Each city has its own mayor and council, with the four mayors meeting regularly to discuss mat-

---

Maori Place Names
Many of Auckland's landmarks and districts, and almost all the islands of the Hauraki Gulf, retain their original Maori names. Their translation reveals much of the isthmus's pre-European history.
Tamaki-makau-rau: The name translates as 'Tamaki [the maiden], contended for by a hundred lovers'.
Waitemata: 'Water as smooth as the surface of obsidian'. Obsidian, or volcanic glass, was mined by Maori in the Bay of Plenty.
Manukau: 'Wading birds'.
Hauraki: 'Northern wind'.
Rangitoto: 'Bleeding sky'. The island's full name is 'Nga Rangi-i-totongia-a-Tama-te-kapua', or 'the days of the bleeding of Tama-te-kapua'. A chief of the Arawa canoe was badly wounded here.
Waitakere: 'Cascading waters' or 'deep pools'. Auckland's Waitakere Range was named after a chief, murdered at the Waitekauri Stream.

OVERVIEW

Peter Siddell (b1935)
The paintings of **Peter Siddell** magically capture the environment of suburban Auckland, where he has lived all his life. His paintings are intensely realistic, blending the isthmus's volcanic cones, harbours and cloudscapes with the villas that are its most distinctive form of domestic architecture. He captures the details of the cones and the embellishments of the villas, while also giving a heightened sense of the combination of natural and man-made features which are an integral part of Auckland. His images are devoid of objects that may blight the landscape: cars, telephone poles, street signs and people. As one critic put it, 'He is a visionary, imagining an idealized Auckland that might have been but never was'.

---

ters concerning Auckland. Although each city has its own character, local loyalties are blurred – the isthmus is too narrow for separateness to be meaningful. To most Aucklanders the civic distinctions mean little, apart from to which council they pay their local taxes (called 'rates').

The People

An influx of immigrants, from the Pacific Islands in the 1970s and '80s and from Asia in the 1990s, has resulted in Auckland becoming a thoroughly multicultural city. The world's largest Polynesian city, 11.6% are Maori, 13.8% Asian and 14% are of Pacific Island descent. Just over 58% of Aucklanders are European. There are also recent immigrant groups from South Africa, India, Somalia, Iraq, Iran, Afghanistan, Russia, Turkey and Croatia.

This has changed the face of Auckland from the predominantly European, English-speaking society that it was in the 1950s to the polyglot, cosmopolitan city that it is today. The ethnic mix has brought a much greater variety of cultural life to Auckland.

There are festivals celebrating the city's diverse cultures, and a great variety of restaurants where the cuisine from almost every ethnicity in the world can be sampled.

Auckland is a favoured destination for New Zealanders from other parts of the country. The 'northward drift', first observed in the 1960s, has continued. It is estimated that three out of four Aucklanders were born in another part of New Zealand.

The Arts

The Arts

Auckland has a thriving arts community. Most of New Zealand's painters, musicians, printmakers, sculptors, glass artists, actors, dancers and writers live and work in the Auckland region, sustained by the country's largest market for their work, grants from the national arts funding body, Creative New Zealand, and local funding bodies. In recent years some exciting indigenous art forms have emerged, blending European and Polynesian elements in form and theme.

Above: *The Auckland Art Gallery Café.*
Opposite: *A warrior in traditional costume performing the haka.*

Auckland's three public art galleries are the **Auckland Museum** (*see* page 14), the **Auckland Art Gallery Toi O Tamaki** (*see* page 39), and the **New Gallery** (*see* page 40).

The main dealer galleries are in the Kitchener-Lorne Street area and in the main streets of suburbs such as Parnell, Ponsonby, Devonport and at Te Tuhi – The Mark at Pakuranga. Other exhibition spaces are at the Lopdell House Gallery in Titirangi, and the Gus Fisher Gallery in the Kenneth Myers Centre (an outpost of the University of Auckland, at 74 Shortland Street). Students of Elam Art School exhibit their work at the George Fraser Gallery, in the Frank Sargeson Centre at the top of Albert Park, and avant-garde art is also exhibited at Artspace, at 300 Karangahape Road. Auckland City's community arts facility, Artstation, is at 1 Ponsonby Road. The restored grand old Lake House Arts Centre, relocated from its original site above Takapuna Beach to 37 Fred Thomas Drive, is also a venue for local art exhibitions.

Auckland's Literature

Many of New Zealand's authors and playwrights live in the Auckland area, notably the North Shore, where there has been a tradition of literary productivity. Nearly all of New Zealand's publishers are also based on the Shore. Books by Auckland writers are available at the city's bookshops. Writers who have incorporated Auckland into their work include poets ARD Fairburn, Bob Orr and Kevin Ireland, novelists Noel Virtue, Peter Wells and Chad Taylor, children's writer Tessa Duder and playwrights Bruce Mason, Toa Fraser, Oscar Kightley and Roger Hall.

HIGHLIGHTS

The Domain
New Zealand's oldest park, the Auckland Domain is 74ha (183 acres) in size and occupies an ancient volcanic mound called by Maori, **Pukekaroa**. Today it includes the War Memorial Museum, cenotaph, the Winter Garden and Fernery, band rotunda and kiosk, formal gardens, duck ponds, mature trees, sportsgrounds and many paths and walkways. The **Winter Garden** has a large collection of temperate and tropical plants. An expanse of greenery between Parnell and the Auckland Hospital, the Domain's gently contoured landscape is loved by Aucklanders for its natural beauty and many recreational purposes. It is here too that free outdoor **concerts** are held every summer, attracting many thousands to the performances under the stars.
☎ (09) 379 2020
🖥 www.akcity.govt.nz

See Map A–E4   ★★★

THE AUCKLAND MUSEUM

The Auckland Museum, which crowns a hill named **Pukekawa** by Maori, in the **Auckland Domain**, is one of the city's outstanding cultural landmarks and a NZ$64.5 million refurbishment was completed in 2006. Although there has been an Auckland Museum for 150 years, the present building was completed in 1929. A treasure trove of New Zealand's history, the imposing neo-classical building houses an outstanding collection of **Polynesian** and **Melanesian** artefacts, along with discovery centres and exhibitions covering every aspect of the nation's history. The exhibition *Scars on the Heart* commemorates New Zealand war history from the land wars of the 19th century through to present-day peacekeeping activities. The museum also has regular Maori cultural performances, and contains a café and souvenir shop. The view from the museum's steps, looking north over the Waitemata Harbour to Devonport and Rangitoto, is one of the best in the city.

The Auckland Museum: ☎ Infoline (09) 306 7067, 🖥 www.aucklandmuseum.com ⊕ daily, 10:00–17:00, admission by donation.

Opposite: *A busy waterfront bar in the Vladuct Harbour, central Auckland.*
Right: *The Auckland Museum stands on a volcanic hill in the Domain.*

14

AUCKLAND MUSEUM & VIADUCT HARBOUR

 See Map A–C1   ★★★

THE VIADUCT HARBOUR

In 1995 Team New Zealand brought home from San Diego the America's Cup, symbol of world sailing supremacy. The team's two defences of the cup, in 2000 and 2003, saw the Waitemata Harbour's waterfront transformed into a place of glamour and entertainment. Although the America's Cup was lost to a Swiss sailing syndicate in 2003, the Viaduct Harbour remains a major leisure and dining precinct.

The base for both the **Louis Vuitton Cup** – to decide which yachting syndicate challenged for the **America's Cup** – and for the cup defence itself, was the Viaduct Harbour. Located between Halsey Street and Princes Wharf, at the western end of Quay Street, the Viaduct Harbour is an enclosed basin for pleasure craft, with a stage area for outdoor concerts, an information centre and a plaza containing shops, bars, cafés, entertainers, sculptural installations and restaurants. A paved **Maritime Trail**, with informative plaques on key aspects of Auckland's nautical history, follows the edge of the viaduct basin, alongside the fishing boats and superyachts. The harbour is a place to stroll, dine and savour the sights of vessels of all types, coming and going on the sparkling **Waitemata Harbour**.

In the summer months, from December to March, the Viaduct Harbour becomes the focus of the busiest and most varied entertainment in Downtown Auckland.

Auckland's Views
Auckland's up-and-down topography offers many vantage points from which to view the isthmus and its harbours. From the tops of the volcanic cones of **Mt Eden**, **One Tree Hill** and **Mt Wellington**, there are commanding views of the city, while on the northern side of the Waitemata Harbour, **North Head** and **Mt Victoria** provide views of the Rangitoto Channel and Hauraki Gulf islands. **JF Kennedy Park** has superb views of the gulf and Rangitoto Island and from the west there are panoramic views of Auckland city from the **Waitakere Ranges** and parts of the **Scenic Drive**. On the eastern waterfront, **Point Resolution** in Parnell and **MJ Savage Memorial** overlook the outer harbour. But the natural view to beat them all is from the summit of **Rangitoto Island** (260m; 850ft), which encompasses the entire Auckland region.

HIGHLIGHTS

See Map A–D2 ★★★

THE SKY TOWER

Since its completion in 1997 the Sky Tower has become a dominant and respected addition to Auckland's skyline. Soaring from the central business district to a height of 328m (1076ft), making it the tallest building in the Southern Hemisphere, the tower contains three viewing levels and a revolving restaurant in its 'pod' at the top. The decks give 360° views of Greater Auckland and most of the Tamaki Isthmus's 49 extinct volcanic vents. Located on the main observation level are 38mm (1.5in) glass floor panels which give dizzying downward views. There is also an interesting audiovisual display documenting the geological and human history of Auckland.

The cones of Auckland's main volcanic hills are nature reserves – from the top of the tower they can be seen standing out from the surrounding built-up landscape like green pyramids. A trip to the top of the Sky Tower provides the visitor with an instant introduction to Auckland's natural and cultural geography.

And for the bold, **Sky Jump** provides the ultimate thrill, a 192m (630ft) bungy jump from the tower. For more information visit: www.skyjump.co.nz

---

The Sky Tower
✉ Corner of Victoria and Federal Streets, central city
☎ (09) 363 6000 or 0800 759 2489
📠 (09) 363 6010
💻 www.skycity.co.nz
🕐 08:30 until late, daily
💰 Adults $20, children 5–14 years $8, under 5 years free. $3 extra for top level platform, 'Skydeck'.
🍽 The Sky City complex, beneath the tower, contains a casino and bars, six restaurants, a theatre, hotel and a convention centre. There is a revolving restaurant at the top of the tower.

SKY TOWER & UNDERWATER WORLD

 See Map B–F1 ★★★

KELLY TARLTON'S ANTARCTIC ENCOUNTER AND UNDERWATER WORLD

Located on Auckland's picturesque eastern waterfront, this attraction enables visitors to observe underwater sea life and a recreation of an Antarctic habitat through a plexiglass tunnel. The aquarium is located in what used to be storage tanks for Auckland's city sewage. Now, conveyed through the tunnel on a moving walkway, people can observe, close-up and in comfort, sharks, stingrays, snapper and other marine inhabitants of the seas around Auckland. It's like taking a stroll along the ocean floor, totally surrounded by the denizens of the deep.

The second attraction here is the colonies of King and Gentoo penguins, which are viewed in their icy habitat from a slow-moving Antarctic snow-cat. Other exhibits enable the visitor to better understand the extreme hardships that the early Antarctic explorers had to endure.

Kelly Tarlton's Antarctic Encounter and Underwater World
✉ 23 Tamaki Drive
☎ 0800 805 050
🖥 www.kellytarltons.co.nz
✉ ktinfo@kellytarltons.co.nz
🕘 09:00–20:00 (summer), 09:00–18:00 (winter), daily
💰 Adults $28, 65 years+ $21 students with ID $21, children 5–15 years $14, under 4 years free, family prices are also available ($47–78).
🍴 Docksiders
☎ (09) 521 3930

Opposite: *The Sky Tower (328m, 1076ft).*
Below: *One of the penguins at Kelly Tarlton's Antarctic Encounter and Underwater World.*

HIGHLIGHTS

Devonport's Literary Heritage
Devonport has been home to many poets, writers and novelists, a tradition which continues to this day. Relishing the district's informality, lovely beaches and ease of access to the city by ferry, Devonport's writers have contributed much to maintaining the suburb's character. Two literary walks incorporating the writers' homes can be taken in the area (details in the booklet *North Shore Literary Walks*, published by North Shore City, available, along with other booklets, from the Information Centre in Victoria Road).

Opposite: *Muriwai, one of Auckland's black sand west-coast beaches.*
Below: *Devonport, Waitemata Harbour and central Auckland as seen from Mount Victoria, Devonport.*

See Map C–E5 / A–D1   ★★★

DEVONPORT BY FERRY

Eleven minutes by ferry across the Waitemata Harbour from the Ferry Building, in Quay Street, is the maritime suburb of Devonport. One of Auckland's earliest harbourside suburbs and since the 1880s the headquarters of the Royal New Zealand Navy, Devonport is today renowned for its shops, restaurants, villas, buildings, and the superb views from its two volcanic cones, **Mount Victoria** and **North Head**.

The ferry passes the naval base at **Calliope Wharf** just before it docks at the **Devonport Wharf**, directly across from the suburb's main street, Victoria Road, which slopes up to Mount Victoria. Beside the wharf is **Windsor Reserve**, where there is a playground and sandy beach, while across the street, surrounding the public library, is a reserve with a huge Moreton Bay fig tree and a band rotunda. In the main street is the grand old Esplanade Hotel, an Information Centre, quality shops, an art gallery, several eateries and three excellent bookshops. A short walk around the eastern waterfront is **Torpedo Bay**, and just a stroll across the other side of the peninsula is **Cheltenham Beach**, a lovely golden sand beach facing the Rangitoto Channel. In the centre of the peninsula, bounded by Albert and Vauxhall Roads, is **Mount Cambria Reserve**, a tranquil park surrounding the remains of another extinct volcano. Ferries to and from Devonport arrive and leave every half hour.

DEVONPORT & WEST COAST BEACHES

See Map D–A5 ★★★

THE WEST COAST BEACHES

The most spectacular landscape in the Auckland region is along its west coast, from **Whatipu** to **Muriwai Beach**. This 20km (12-mile) stretch contains the black sand beaches of Karekare,

Piha, Anawhata, Te Henga (Bethells) and Muriwai, where huge waves crash down after being driven in from the Tasman Sea by prevailing west and southwest winds.

The black sand of the west coast beaches is composed of magnetic iron oxide from the remains of a volcano in Taranaki province, to the south, and swept up the coast by wind and ocean currents. Above the beaches are cliffs of conglomerated rock, evidence of volcanic eruptions dating back 20 million years. The cliffs have been sculpted – in some places into vast caves – by wind and waves. Behind many beaches are sand dunes and stands of windswept tussock, manuka and pohutukawa.

The west coast is a land and seascape of awesome grandeur, one which dwarfs the human visitor. For these reasons the area has been used as a setting for several films and television series, including *Black Beauty*, *The Piano*, *Xena* and *Hercules*.

Swimming is possible at all the west coast beaches, but the strength of the waves and the sea currents (called 'rips' here), make it a very dangerous stretch of water. Only swim between the red and yellow flags, which indicate the areas patrolled by lifeguards, and always be alert for rogue waves.

Karekare Beach
One of the most ruggedly beautiful beaches on Auckland's west coast is Karekare. Reached by a road which branches from the main road across the Waitakeres to Piha, Karekare lies at the foot of steep cliffs, down which cascades a lovely waterfall, a short walk from the carpark. A stream flows across the black sand beach, in the centre of which is a huge headland which can be climbed, giving panoramic views of Karekare and the Tasman Sea. Behind the beach are sand dunes and a lovely grove of pohutukawa trees. Swimming is possible in Karekare's turbulent surf, but must be confined to the lifeguard patrolled area, indicated by red and yellow flags. At low tide exhilarating walks can be taken south along Karekare beach, past spectacular cliff formations, all the way to Whatipu.

HIGHLIGHTS

Boat Charters
In summer, there are ample opportunities to get out on the waters of the Waitemata Harbour. It's possible to sail on a genuine former America's Cup yacht, NZL40 or NZL41, the tall ship *Soren Larsen*, a vintage tug boat or steam boat, a luxury charter yacht, a schooner, a catamaran or a water taxi. A ride on one of the Devonport or Hauraki Gulf island ferries also provides a close-up of the harbour. Most charters leave from the Viaduct Harbour or the steps to the left of the Ferry Building. The Pride of Auckland sailing and dining cruises leave from the harbour frontage of the Maritime Museum. To see the harbour upfront and personal, try a water taxi. These 16-seater yellow boats do tours of the Viaduct Harbour as well as ferrying customers to wherever they want to get to, including Waiheke Island. For trips on the harbour in various vessels, phone 0800 936 306.
🖳 www.viaductvoyager.co.nz
🖳 www.yellowboat.co.nz
🖳 www.sailnewzealand.co.nz
🖳 www.prideofauckland.com
🖳 www.sorenlarson.co.nz

See Map A–D1   ★★

THE NEW ZEALAND NATIONAL MARITIME MUSEUM
Adjacent to the Viaduct Harbour is the National Maritime Museum, corner Quay and Hobson Streets, containing 14 exhibition halls displaying New Zealand's age-old relationship with the sea. Exhibits include a traditional double-hulled, Polynesian ocean-voyaging canoe, the cabin of a 19th-century immigrant sailing ship which recreates the rolling of the sea, and a typical Kiwi bach (seaside holiday cottage) from the 1950s. There are also computer lists of immigrants to New Zealand. Next to the museum, moored along the wharf, are preserved sailing and steam-powered vessels from New Zealand's maritime history. Public sailings on modern yachts can be taken from just in front of the museum (*see* side panel). A visit to this museum provides a unique and fascinating experience. ☎ Infoline: (09) 373 0800, 🖳 www.nzmaritime.org ⊕ daily, 09:00–18:00.

MARITIME MUSEUM & ALBERT PARK

See Map A–D2/3 ★★

ALBERT PARK

Only a short walk uphill from Auckland's main street, Queen Street, is Albert Park. Bounded by Kitchener, Princes and Wellesley Streets and Bowen Avenue, Albert Park lies directly opposite the campus of the **University of Auckland**, and is an oasis for students and city workers alike. Crisscrossed by footpaths which converge at a pond at its top, the park is filled with mature trees and has statues of 19th-century politician Sir George Grey and Queen Victoria. There is also a Victorian band rotunda at the southern end of the park. At the southwest corner is the **Auckland Art Gallery**, and at 25A Princes Street is the **Frank Sargeson Centre**, which incorporates the **George Fraser Gallery**, where students of Elam Art School exhibit their work. Restful at any time of the year, Albert Park is particularly lovely in spring and autumn, when its deciduous trees look glorious.

Albert Park
This park is two streets east of Queen Street, and a short walk up Victoria Street East. The striking sculpture by Chris Booth, *Gateways*, beside the corner of Bowen Avenue and Kitchener Street, consists of twin towers of piled basalt boulders, connected at the top by a steel archway. The park is open all hours, but should be explored during daylight hours only and not entered alone after dark.

City Art Gallery
✉ Corner Wellesley and Kitchener Streets
☎ (09) 307 7700
📠 (09) 302 1096
💻 www.aucklandcity.govt.nz/artgallery
🕐 10:00–17:00, daily
💰 The ground-floor gallery is free, special exhibitions are $12–15
🍽 Café

George Fraser Gallery
✉ 25A Princes Street
☎ (09) 367 7163
🕐 11:00–16:00 Wed–Fri, 11:00–14:00 Sat
💰 Free

Opposite: *The New Zealand National Maritime Museum on the waterfront, Waitemata Harbour.*
Left: *Albert Park, the University of Auckland's Clock Tower (centre) and Auckland Museum (top right).*

HIGHLIGHTS

The Museum of Transport and Technology
✉ Great North Road, Western Springs
☎ (09) 846 0199
📠 (09) 846 4242
💻 www.motat.org.nz
🕐 10:00–17:00, daily

✪ *See* Map B–D2   ★★

THE MUSEUM OF TRANSPORT AND TECHNOLOGY (MOTAT)

For those fascinated by the evolution of technology, MOTAT provides a unique opportunity to observe the way New Zealand's transport and communications have changed over the centuries. Located at Western Springs, where the city's first water supply originated, this special museum includes the restored 1877 pumphouse and its enormous beam engine – one of only three such working beam engines in the world – along with vintage cars, tramcars, a Wellerhaus fairground organ, a 'hands-on' science area and a re-creation of a colonial village high street. There is also a model of the 1903 aeroplane in which New Zealand pioneer aviator Richard Pearse achieved powered flight, some claim before the Wright brothers managed to do so.

For another interesting experience, take a trip on the restored tram that runs every 20 minutes from MOTAT's Great North Road entrance to the Auckland Zoo and back.

Sir Keith Park Memorial Site
The second of MOTAT's two display sites, this exhibition hangar in Meola Road, also accessible from Motions Road, contains an impressive display of historic aircraft, including the only remaining Solent Mark IV flying boat in the world. During the 1940s and '50s Auckland's air connections with the rest of the world depended on the Solent 'flying boats' which linked the city with Sydney and South Pacific islands such as Fiji, Samoa, Aitutaki in the Cook Islands, and Tahiti. At the memorial site there is also an Avro Lancaster Bomber, Sunderland and Fleet Air Arm displays, and rail exhibits and memorabilia. The exhibits here are all maintained by voluntary labour.

MOTAT & AUCKLAND ZOO

See Map B–D1   ★★

AUCKLAND ZOO

Auckland Zoo is a favourite place for people of all ages. Within its spacious grounds are fauna and flora from all over the world.

The animals are housed in open enclosures, permitting them to roam in relative freedom and visitors to study the creatures in recreations of their natural environment. Giraffes, zebras, lions and springboks can be seen in the African enclosure, and siamang gibbons, spider monkeys and tamarins can be observed in the tropical rainforest area. The zoo is drained by a stream, along whose banks flamingos step and the waters of which provide a home for hippos. Another highlight is a 'coastal journey' through the zoo's Sealion and Penguin Shores, where sealions and penguins can be seen through an underwater window. In the native aviary, many of New Zealand's indigenous birds are on display in a native forest setting.

Two of New Zealand's rarest creatures can be viewed in the Wilderness New Zealand house. The **kiwi**, New Zealand's national symbol even though it is a highly endangered species, and the **tuatara**, an ancient reptile found in the wild only on small islands around the coast, can both be viewed at the zoo's recreated nocturnal forest habitat. This is the only place that many people are able to see these two unique creatures.

Above: *The Great Spotted Kiwi is a nocturnal-foraging bird.*
Opposite: *The tram that runs from outside MOTAT to the Auckland Zoo.*

Auckland Zoo
✉ Motions Road, near Western Springs (by car about five minutes from Downtown – take the North-Western Motorway and exit at Western Springs).
☎ Zoo information line: (09) 360 3819, for a bus phone Rideline: (09) 366 6400
💻 www.aucklandzoo.co.nz
🕘 09:30–17:30, daily (except Christmas Day)
🍽 Café and picnic areas within the zoo grounds

HIGHLIGHTS

✪ See Map D–B5 ★★

THE WAITAKERE RANGES

An hour's drive west of Auckland city is the wilderness area of the Waitakere Ranges Regional Park. Formed from volcanic eruptions millions of years ago, the Waitakeres are an enormous uplifted block of ridges, valleys and peaks averaging over 300m (985ft) above the Tasman Sea, which sweeps along its western coastline. The ranges are covered in regenerating forest after widespread milling removed most of the trees between the 1880s and 1920s. Today there are some remnant stands of kauri, rimu, northern rata, tawa, rewarewa and nikau palms in the podocarp-broadleaf subtropical rainforest. There are waterfalls, streams, wildlife and 250km (155 miles) of walking and tramping tracks. Four roads cross the ranges, providing access to the tracks and black sand beaches which form the Waitakeres' western boundary. To the south are the reservoirs which contain Auckland city's main source of fresh water.

To pre-European Maori, the Waitakeres and surrounding coast were a rich source of food. With the arrival of Europeans, the forests were milled heavily. Today the Waitakeres are protected, their resources conserved for both present and future generations.

The **Waitakere Tramline Society** offers a narrow-gauge diesel train tour through part of the Waitakeres, on Sundays, giving views of the forest and the Waitakere Falls. Trips by bookings only: ☎ (09) 836 0900 or (09) 818 4946, 💻 www.waitakere tramline.org.nz

---

<u>Arataki Environmental & Heritage Centre</u>
A visit to the Waitakere Ranges should start at this centre, at the southern end of Scenic Drive, which runs along the eastern side of the ranges. 'Arataki' means 'pathway to learning', and as such the centre contains displays illustrating the geological, botanical and human characteristics of the ranges, from the first occupation by Maori through to the present day. Carvings by Maori artists are a special feature, notably the pou or guardian pole at its entrance. A shop sells souvenirs, maps and other publications on the Waitakeres.
Around the centre are walkways and platforms which provide sweeping views of the Waitakeres and the Manukau Harbour.
✉ Highway 24 (Scenic Drive), 6km (3.7 miles) past Titirangi village
☎ Parksline: (09) 303 1530
💻 www.arc.govt.nz
🕘 09:00–17:00, daily

WAITAKERE RANGES & REGIONAL PARKS

 See Map D–C3/4, D6   ★★

AUCKLAND'S REGIONAL PARKS

Within a relatively short distance of Auckland city are 25 regional parks, areas of outstanding natural beauty close to, or beside, the west and east coast beaches. Maintained by the Auckland Regional Council, these parks have ample provision for picnicking and barbecueing, as well as toilets and changing facilities. The largest of the parks is the **Hunua Ranges Regional Park**, to the southeast of the Auckland isthmus, the second largest the **Waitakere Ranges** and its adjacent west coast beaches. Beach parks include **Awhitu**, on the southern peninsula of the Manukau Harbour, **Shakespear** on the Whangaparaoa Peninsula, **Long Bay** and **Wenderholm**. The parks offer almost endless recreational possibilities: swimming, picnicking, kayaking, tramping and mountain biking. Campsites are available in parks throughout the region, and special events are held regularly at the various parks. These include voluntary tree and native grass planting, gardening discovery programmes and special interest walks.

For detailed information call Parksline ☎ (09) 303 1530 or visit 🖳 www.arc.govt.nz

> **Muriwai's Gannet Colony**
> At the southern end of Muriwai Beach, on a fenced-off cliff-top and a rocky islet above Maori Bay, a thriving colony of Australasian gannets (*Morus serrator*) can be seen. These graceful, yellow-headed birds are noted for their spectacular vertical diving from great heights into the sea to catch fish. They lay their eggs directly onto the rocks on the cliff-top and atop a neighbouring stack – a tall, sheer-sided island – where their chicks hatch and are fed by their parents. The eggs are laid from July until October. Then, at the end of the New Zealand summer, the young gannets fly to Australia before returning to Muriwai to breed. A walkway leads from the southern end of the beach and up the cliff to a viewing area from where the birds can be observed.

Opposite: *A view of the Waitakere Ranges from outside the Arataki Environmental and Heritage Centre.*
Left: *Shakespear Regional Park, on the Whangaparaoa Peninsula.*

HIGHLIGHTS

⭐ See Map C–D1	★★

LONG BAY REGIONAL PARK

Aptly named Long Bay lies on Auckland's North Shore, at the northern end of North Shore City. A long straight stretch of sandy beach, Long Bay's foreshore is lined with trees, sand dunes and an expanse of grass which forms the perfect location for a picnic lunch. There is also a children's playground above the beach. **Swimming** at Long Bay is excellent – the beach is safe and the water can be enjoyed at all tides. For those who enjoy **walking**, a pathway which climbs the cliff at the beach's northern end extends all the way along the cliff-top to the tidal estuary of the **Okura River**. There is also a marine reserve from Long Bay to the Okura estuary.

Excellent bush and coastal walks can be undertaken on the northern side of the estuary, in the Okura Scenic Reserve, reached via East Coast Road and Haigh Access Road.

Auckland Regional Botanic Gardens
Located adjacent to the Southern Motorway near Manurewa, this horticultural haven covering 64ha (158 acres) is home to more than 10,000 different plants ranging from New Zealand native species to exotics from all the world's continents, as well as the other islands of the South Pacific. Extensive plantings of special gardens include roses, herbs, magnolias and camellias, while at the northern end of the gardens is a 30ha (74 acre) broadleaf and podocarp forest remnant. Special programmes and demonstrations are held at the gardens during the year. Best-known of these is the **Ellerslie Flower Show**, the annual showcase for New Zealand's horticultural diversity and achievements. It is usually held in mid-November.
✉ Travelling south by car, take the Manurewa off-ramp, turn left into Hill Road and drive along to the entrance on the left.
☎ (09) 309 7875 or Parksline: (09) 303 1530
🕗 08:00 to dusk, daily

Right: *Long Bay beach, on the North Shore, is popular for swimming and picnicking.*

Long Bay & Waitemata Waterfront

 See Map A–C1 to F1　★★

THE WAITEMATA WATERFRONT

Auckland city's front doorstep is the southern waterfront of the Waitemata Harbour. Extending several kilometres from the **Viaduct Harbour** to **St Heliers**, this stretch of waterfront takes in, from west to east: the Viaduct Harbour, the New Zealand National Maritime Museum, the Princes Wharf complex, the Ferry Building and ferry terminals, and the wharves between Queens Wharf and Mechanics Bay. After that are Hobson Bay and the Okahu Bay boat harbour before the road passes beneath Paratai Drive, past the Orakei Domain and Okahu Bay, around the point under which Kelly Tarlton's Antarctic Encounter and Underwater World is located, beneath MJ Savage Memorial Park and around Bastion Point to Mission Bay and St Heliers.

Quay Street merges with Tamaki Drive to trace the coastline along the waterfront, and beside the road is a walkway, also used for cycling and rollerblading. Alongside this is the Waitemata Harbour, with scores of yachts, launches, ferries and board sailors, while still in sight are the high-rise buildings of the central business district. Across the harbour, Devonport can be seen, with its navy base, villas and the two volcanic cones of Mount Victoria and North Head.

From Mission Bay and St Heliers is an unimpeded view of the Rangitoto Channel and Rangitoto Island itself, a massive green monolith and the newest of the Auckland region's 49 volcanoes.

Above: *Prince's Wharf, Waitemata Harbour.*

Mission Bay

The beachside suburb of Mission Bay lies adjacent to a sweep of golden sand, a promenade and a large reserve on the shores of the Waitemata Harbour. At the western end of the reserve is the historic Mission House, built from stone brought in the 1850s from Rangitoto, the volcanic island which dominates the skyline across from the beach. A little further along in the reserve is a fountain which plays regularly. Mission Bay itself is perfectly safe for swimming or picnicking, while across the Promenade is a great array of cafés and restaurants where lunches or evening meals can be taken. Superb harbour views can be enjoyed along with the cuisine.
🖥 www.missionbay.co.nz

HIGHLIGHTS

Right: *The Central City Library, in Lorne Street, is Auckland's largest.*
Opposite: *Cornwall Park, donated to the city by its 'founding father', Sir John Logan Campbell, today provides extensive recreational areas.*

See Map A–D2 ★★

CENTRAL CITY LIBRARY

Auckland caters well to bibliophiles. Along with its many retail bookshops, the city has excellent council-operated community libraries in all its suburbs and a large one, the Central City Library, in Lorne Street, one street east of Queen Street. The Central City Library is spread over three escalator-connected floors. The ground floor holds Fiction, Biography and Languages, CDs and Books Out Loud; Floor 1 Business, Economics and Children's books, and Floor 2 is given over to heritage literature. The Heritage floor contains the Auckland Research Centre, which has a vast collection of European and Polynesian material, and the library's Special Collections room. The latter – one of the city's heritage gems – holds New Zealand's largest collection of Shakespeare and medieval manuscripts, several pre-16th-century printed books and the only books in New Zealand printed by William Caxton. The library also holds 7000 historic maps and half a million photographs.

Central City Library
Overseas visitors can use the Central City Library facilities by taking out a special 'Bond Membership', on presentation of their passport and proof of a current local residential address.
✉ 44–46 Lorne Street
☎ (09) 377 0209
📠 (09) 307 7741
💻 www.aucklandcitylibraries.com
🕘 09:30–20:00 Mon–Fri, 10:00–16:00 Sat, 12:00–16:00 Sun

CITY LIBRARY & CORNWALL PARK

See Map B–E2 ★

CORNWALL PARK

Presented to the people of Auckland in 1901 by the city's 'founding father', Sir John Logan Campbell, Cornwall Park is, in the Victorian businessman and philanthropist's words, 'a place of public resort for the recreation and enjoyment of the people of New Zealand'. Today, make that 'of people from everywhere'. Cornwall Park is a rural oasis bounded by busy highways and incessant traffic. Just to turn into one of the several broad avenues which cross the park is to immediately enter a purely pastoral world, one where sheep and cattle graze, where there are groves of mature specimen trees, walls of volcanic stone and walking paths, and whose slopes rise to the summit of **One Tree Hill**, the site of Logan Campbell's grave and one of Auckland's most prominent natural landmarks. Called Maungakiekie by Maori, the summit of this complex volcanic cone affords glorious views of the suburbs of Ellerslie, Epsom and Royal Oak and more distant parts of the Tamaki isthmus. The pine tree that gave One Tree Hill its name was vandalized in 1994, and is to be replaced with a native tree. One of Campbell's preserved houses, **Acacia Cottage**, lies at the northern foot of One Tree Hill, on Olive Grove Drive, directly opposite the kiosk.

> **Stardome Observatory**
> Situated on the lower southern slopes of One Tree Hill, the Stardome offers a spectacular introduction to the southern skies, including the Southern Cross, Alpha Centauri – the closest star to our solar system – the Milky Way and our nearest galactic neighbours, the Large and Small Magellanic Clouds. In the Stardome's Planetarium an all-sky, 360° panoramic theatre offers a multimedia experience with special effects projectors and digital surround sound. Large telescope viewing of the night sky is also available, subject to weather conditions.
> ✉ One Tree Hill Domain, off Manukau Road, Royal Oak
> ☎ (09) 624 1246
> 🖥 www.stardome.org.nz
> ✉ info@stardome.org.nz
> 🕐 Daily

HIGHLIGHTS

○ *See* Map A–D6 | ★

MOUNT EDEN

Highest of the Tamaki isthmus's volcanic cones, Mount Eden Domain is a delightful reserve just a few minutes' drive (or a steep climb) from Mount Eden village. A one-way road spirals around the verdant slopes of the extinct volcano, and from a viewing area at the summit the city of Auckland spreads in all directions. The grassy, steep-sided crater within the mountain is like a huge natural amphitheatre, at the bottom of which is a scattering of scoria rubble – a remnant of the lava which provides a reminder of the mountain's volcanic birth 20,000 years earlier. The upper slopes of the cone contain easily recognizable food storage pits and trenches, relics of the mountain's pre-European Maori inhabitants, who called the cone Maungawhau, or 'hill of the whau', the latter being a plant which grew on its slopes and whose pods Maori used as floats for their fishing nets.

Mount Eden village is a very pleasant suburb of gentrified Victorian villas and leafy streets. The village and shops lie along Mount Eden Road, at the western foot of the mountain. The main street has a range of quality food shops, cafés, restaurants, salons and a book store. The streets running west from Mount Eden Road all lead to the north–south arterial route of Dominion Road.

Eden Garden
At the eastern foot of Mount Eden lies one of Auckland's best-kept secrets, Eden Garden. Reached via Omana Avenue, off Mountain Road, Eden Garden was once a quarry whose scoria helped build the city. After the quarry was abandoned in 1928, it was converted into a garden. Today it is a complex of native and exotic plants and shrubs – and the most varied camellia collection in New Zealand – connected by a maze of pathways. The garden rises to the base of a cliff of scoria and a lookout with city and harbour views.
☎ (09) 638 8395
🖥 www.edengarden.co.nz
🕓 10:00–16:00, daily
🍽 Café in the garden

Below: *Tourists gather at the summit of the Mount Eden Domain to enjoy extensive views.*

MOUNT EDEN & PARNELL ROAD

See Map A–F3 ★

PARNELL ROAD

Astride a ridge just east of the Domain and rising steeply from the waterfront, Parnell was Auckland city's first settled suburb. It has retained its colonial ambience in spite of 160 years of urban development and the decay which beset the area during the 1950s and '60s. Today **Parnell Road** is shamelessly upmarket, epitomizing the colonial chic side of Auckland city, while on either side of this main thoroughfare restored Victorian cottages and villas stand cheek-by-jowl with modern townhouses and apartments. Parnell Road has become synonymous with fine restaurants and pavement cafés, shopping boutiques and, in particular, fine art galleries. There is a Parnell Art Gallery walk, which gives details of every gallery in the area.

Only a short walk from the southern end of Parnell Road are the historic buildings of St Mary's Church, the Kinder House, Ewelme Cottage and the Jubilee Building, while to the north of Parnell is Dove Meyer Robinson Park with its superb seasonal rose display. A short walk east of this park, just off Judges Bay Road, is an exquisite colonial church, St Stephen's Chapel (1856), which stands alone above Judges Bay, surrounded by a 19th-century graveyard. Also visit www.parnell.net.nz

Above: *Restaurants off Parnell Road, an upmarket shopping street.*

The Parnell Seawater Baths

These renovated seawater baths, Auckland's oldest, are on the Waitemata waterfront, reached from the south by Judges Bay Road or St Stephens Avenue, which converge on Point Resolution Park, or from the harbour side by a footbridge over Tamaki Drive. Set below the park, under the sandstone cliffs which are a feature of the Waitemata Waterfront, the open-air Parnell Seawater Baths have a picturesque location and are ideal for a refreshing stopover while walking, cycling or roller-blading along Tamaki Drive.

HIGHLIGHTS

Right: *Ponsonby Road is one of Auckland's longest and busiest shopping streets.*

> ⊛ See Map A–A2   ★

Ponsonby Road

Ponsonby Road extends from the Three Lamps shopping centre at its northern end to the intersection with Karangahape Road at its southern end, a total distance of 1.7km (1 mile). Ponsonby Road is lined with antique shops, gift shops, book shops, food stores, coffee bars, home decorating shops, fashion boutiques, salons, cafés and restaurants to suit all tastes. Most of the banks and food retailers are at the Three Lamps end of Ponsonby Road, while across the intersection with College Hill, at 1 St Marys Bay Road, is the historic Ponsonby Post Office building. A little further along St Marys Bay Road, at number 20, is the equally venerable and historic Leys Institute, Ponsonby's community library.
The best public transport to Ponsonby Road from outside the Britomart Centre is via the 015 and 199 Stagecoach buses, or the Link bus. Details on MAXX:
☎ (09) 366 6400 or
🖳 www.maxx.co.nz

PONSONBY

Parnell's equivalent on the western side of the Queen Street valley is Ponsonby, another Victorian suburb which has been gentrified in recent decades. The main thoroughfare of this suburb, Ponsonby Road, runs from Karangahape Road at its southern end to Jervois (locally pronounced 'Jer-voice') Road at its northern end. Running off both sides of Ponsonby Road are narrow streets closely packed with 19th-century villas and cottages. Where Ponsonby Road meets Jervois Road is the busy Three Lamps shopping centre, just before which is historic Renall Street, a heritage street filled with protected colonial cottages.

A stroll up one side of busy, stylish Ponsonby Road and down the other takes at least half a day, with a latte or lunch at one of the pavement cafés an optional extra. Jervois Road, reached after a left turn at Ponsonby Road's northern end, continues Ponsonby's theme of quality dining and drinking, with many excellent cafés and restaurants lining the southern side of the road.

PONSONBY & TITIRANGI

See Map B–B4   ★

TITIRANGI

Auckland's leafiest suburb, Titirangi, translates as 'the fringe of heaven'. Located atop steep hills above the northern shores of the Manukau Harbour, Titirangi's shopping area has a truly 'village' aspect to it. Clustered around the highest part of **Titirangi Road** is a collection of shops, cafés and restaurants, and slightly further, where the road becomes the Waitakeres' Scenic Drive, is the strikingly styled **Lopdell House**, which contains art galleries and a theatre.

Titirangi is most notable for the stands of mature native trees which clothe the entire suburb. Kauri, rimu, rata, totara and kanuka trees cover the hills and surround the houses, many of which are hardly visible from the streets. The streets radiate in a southerly direction from the central Titirangi village and lead down to a row of secluded, bush-fringed beaches: Davies Bay, Paturoa Bay, French Bay and Wood Bay. There are also several bush-clad reserves in the district.

Southwest of Titirangi, along Huia Road, is **Cornwallis Park** and, extending into the Manukau Harbour, scenic Cornwallis peninsula. A short walk along the peninsula leads to a memorial for the 189 victims of the steam corvette *Orpheus*, which foundered in 1863 at the entrance to the Manukau Harbour – New Zealand's worst sea disaster. Further along the coastal drive, at the end of Whatipu Road, is the windswept, sandy expanse of **Whatipu**, located below the soaring, southernmost peaks of the Waitakere Ranges.

Titirangi
Half an hour's drive southwest of the central city, Titirangi is reached via Great North Road and Ash and Rata Streets, Avondale, which lead into Titirangi Road, beginning on the south side of New Lynn. From there the road climbs steadily to Titirangi village.

Art Gallery
✉ Lopdell House, 418 Titirangi Road
☎ (09) 817 8087
📞 (09) 817 3340
💻 www.lopdell.org.nz
🕐 10:00–16:00, daily

Below: *The distinctive architecture of Lopdell House, Titirangi. The building houses an art gallery and a theatre.*

•SIGHTSEEING

Right: *Takapuna Beach is one of the city's longest.*

Takapuna by the Sea

Takapuna, a large affluent suburb and shopping area on the North Shore, lies adjacent to Takapuna Beach. A glorious expanse of golden sand over a kilometre in length, overlooked in parts by pohutukawa trees, this beach is a favourite location for walking, swimming and picnicking. The beach has unimpeded views of Rangitoto Island and a boat ramp provides access to the Rangitoto Channel and the Hauraki Gulf. The shopping area is only a short stroll up from the beach, and in Takapuna's main street, Hurstmere Road, there are many cafés, bars, restaurants and shops. The Takapuna Market is in the carpark between Hurstmere Road and Lake Road, on Sunday from early until noon. Hotels and motels in the area cater for visitors who prefer to be away from the central city. At off-peak periods it is only ten minutes by car or bus from Takapuna to Queen Street.

Takapuna Visitor Information Centre:
✉ 49 Hurstmere Road
☎ (09) 486 8670
📠 (09) 486 8562
🕐 08:30–17:00

The North Shore

Physically separated from the central city but connected by the harbour bridge, Auckland's North Shore is somewhat removed from the rest of the metropolis. **North Shore City** extends from **Devonport** in the south to **Albany** in the north and encompasses the seaside suburbs known as **East Coast Bays**. Although it mainly consists of recent developments, two suburbs, Devonport and Northcote, are among Auckland's oldest settled districts, dating back to the 1850s. The proximity of the sea and its separateness from the city has encouraged a relaxed way of life on 'the Shore', as it is popularly known. But the area also has, along with historic neighbourhoods and sheltered beaches, sprawling suburbs, shopping malls and industrial parks, and is bisected by the Northern Motorway. Peak-hour traffic congestion on the bridge's feeder roads is considered to be the only disadvantage to living on 'the Shore'.

East Coast Bays

From Takapuna north to Long Bay is the area known as East Coast Bays. Largely a holiday district during the first half of the 20th century, its simple 'baches' (holiday homes) have been replaced by permanent

EAST COAST BAYS

houses and apartments. Although extensive suburbs back the houses and shops, the bays are still beautiful. From south to north they are: **Thorne Bay**, near Takapuna, **Milford**, **Castor Bay**, **Campbells Bay**, **Mairangi Bay**, **Murrays Bay**, **Rothesay Bay**, **Browns Bay**, **Torbay** and **Long Bay**. Only minutes apart along East Coast Bays Road, each bay has a distinctive character. Milford has a picturesque marina, Murrays Bay a jetty, and Castor Bay is overlooked by an ancient *pa* site and reserve. Some, like tiny Thorne Bay and Waiake Beach at Torbay, are accessible only on foot, while others like Browns Bay and Mairangi Bay are much bigger and are backed by large shopping centres. All the bays are safe for swimming and most have boat launching ramps and grassy reserves containing picnic and barbecue areas. In summer the bays are highly popular and crowded, but from March to December they are tranquil and idyllic.

Lake Pupuke

Between Takapuna and Milford is Lake Pupuke, a large lake occupying a deep crater created by a volcanic explosion. The lake is accessible at several places: Killarney Park, Kitchener Park, Sylvan Park and Henderson

> **Auckland's Forests**
> Although most of the native forest which once clothed the Auckland area has been felled to make way for urban and rural developments, some tracts or pockets of forest remain or are regenerating. Largest of these is the vast **Waitakere Ranges**, west of the city, but there are smaller remnants of forest at places like the **Okura Scenic Reserve**, north of Torbay, **Kauri Point Centennial Park**, south of Chatswood, **Le Roys Bush** in Birkenhead and **Smiths Bush** at Onewa Reserve, Takapuna. All these reserves are on the North Shore. Among the forest remnants on the city side are **Bishop Park Scenic Reserve** and **Atkinson Park**, both in Titirangi, **Manurewa Native Bush Reserve**, in Manurewa East, and the **Auckland Regional Botanic Gardens**, next to the Southern Motorway at Manurewa. All these pockets of protected native forest contain well-formed walking tracks.

Left: *The renovated Victorian Pump House (built 1905), beside Lake Pupuke in Takapuna, provides a space for art exhibitions and plays.*

SIGHTSEEING

The Bruce Mason Centre
This is North Shore City's premier performing arts centre and is a popular venue for the performing arts, trade displays, gala dinners and conventions. It was named after New Zealand playwright and actor Bruce Mason (1921–82), who spent his boyhood near Takapuna Beach.
✉ Located on the corner of Hurstmere Road and the Promenade, in the heart of Takapuna
☎ (09) 488 2940
💻 www.bmcentre.co.nz
🍽 The centre is just a few minutes' stroll from the beach, the main shopping area and a row of restaurants and cafés.

Below: *A takahe, one of New Zealand's rarest flightless birds that was long thought to be extinct, ranges freely on Tiritiri Matangi Island in the Hauraki Gulf.*

Park. These parks make agreeable picnic and barbecue areas, and the historic **Pump House** in Killarney Park is used for theatre performances and art exhibitions. Lake Pupuke is popular for sailing, kayaking, windsurfing and angling. The waters seep beneath the volcanic rock land bridge occupied by Hurstmere Road, to emerge as fresh water springs at Thorne Bay.

The Hauraki Gulf and its Islands

Along with the isthmus's preserved volcanic cones, the Hauraki Gulf is Auckland's most beautiful natural asset. The gulf, an inlet of which is the Waitemata Harbour, includes the Whangaparaoa Peninsula, and Rangitoto, Tiritiri Matangi, Little Barrier and Waiheke Islands, to mention a few of its attractions. In between are scores of islands, some relatively undiscovered, like Rakino, which has excellent walks and beaches, and Motuihe, which has safe swimming and fascinating historical associations. Separating the islands are sheltered waterways such as the Tamaki Strait and Rangitoto Channel. World famous due to the America's Cup, the Hauraki Gulf is a nautical nirvana for fishermen, conservationists, sailors and hikers. One of Auckland's most glorious spectacles is the gulf on the annual regatta day when it becomes a place of spectacular maritime beauty and excitement. The gulf is also home to dolphins and whales, which can be observed from chartered launches. Most of

RANGITOTO ISLAND

the islands in the gulf are part of the **Hauraki Gulf Marine Park**, which is open to the public. Access to the islands can be on private pleasure craft or via a regular ferry from the Downtown terminal.

Above: *A view of Rangitoto Island.*

Rangitoto Island

Rangitoto (260m; 853ft) is Auckland's newest and largest volcano, and appears to guard the eastern entrance to the Waitemata Harbour. Probably no more than 650 years old, this basaltic lava volcano last erupted in the 18th century, sending Maori inhabitants of adjoining (and non-volcanic) Motutapu Island hurrying for shelter. Today the landscape is one of extensive scoria fields, covered with pohutukawa trees and epiphytes. There are a few baches (holiday cottages) on the island, but these are disappearing as their leases are not permitted to be renewed. Several tracks cross the island and converge on the summit, from where there are magnificent views of the Hauraki Gulf and Auckland city. The climb to the summit is testing but rewarding. Strong walking shoes are essential, as are supplies of water, because temperatures become very high in summer. For those less fit, a 'summit safari' vehicle takes visitors nearly to the top of the volcano. There is a black sand beach on the island's western side, and swimming is possible in Islington Bay, between Rangitoto and Motutapu. Rangitoto is served by daily ferry connections from the Downtown terminal.

Castor Bay

Castor Bay lies just across the mouth of the tidal Wairau Creek from much larger Milford Beach. Sheltered by sandstone headlands at both ends, the bay is a popular launching place for small yachts and, because of its complete safety, for children's swimming and family picnics on the pretty reserve above the sand. On the northern headland of the bay is Rahopara Pa, an historic reserve covered in mature native trees. A walking track leads up from the beach, through the reserve and north along the cliff-top to JF Kennedy Memorial Park, from where there are panoramic views of Rangitoto Island and the Hauraki Gulf.

SIGHTSEEING

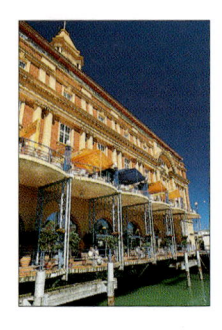

Above: The historic Ferry Building (1912) now accommodates two restaurants.

Historic Northcote
Northcote Point, the North Shore suburb closest to the harbour bridge, is also one of Auckland's oldest. Connected to the city solely by boat for more than a century, until the bridge was opened in 1959, Northcote Point contains many colonial buildings, some of which lie in the shadow of the bridge and its approach roads. A heritage trail around the area has over 30 places of interest, including former shops, an historic tavern, Victorian villas and the wharf at Northcote Point. The walk can be taken with the guidance of an informative booklet, *Northcote Point Walk*, produced by North Shore City Council and available from the local Information Centres.

Historic Buildings

Although modern development has obliterated much of Auckland's colonial history, some stunning houses have been preserved for the public to see how 19th-century European settlers lived. $3 to visit each house below, children free.

Ewelme Cottage

This cottage dates back to 1863, when it was built out of kauri for Rev Vicesimus Lush and his wife. The garden contains an oak tree planted in 1866 and the cottage is filled with family furniture and possessions, including over 800 books.
✉ 14 Ayr Street, Parnell,
☎ / ✆ (09) 379 0202,
⏱ Fri–Sun.

Highwic

Highwic was begun in 1862 by Alfred Buckland, a successful auctioneer, farmer and stock and station agent who fathered 21 children. Located in the shadow of the Newmarket motorway, Highwic has vertical boarding, slate roofs, some latticed windows and kauri-panelled rooms. It is surrounded by a hectare (2.5 acres) of lawns and gardens.
✉ 40 Gillies Avenue, Epsom,
☎ (09) 524 5729,
✆ (09) 524 5575,
⏱ 10:30–12:00, 13:00–16:30 Wed–Sun.

Alberton

Built as a farmhouse in 1863, Alberton was later expanded to 18 rooms, with ornate verandahs and towers. It was owned by the Kerr Taylors, a leading Mount Albert family. In the 19th century Alberton was renowned for its balls, hunts, garden parties and music.
✉ 100 Mt Albert Road, Mt Albert,
☎ (09) 846 7367,
✆ (09) 846 1919,
⏱ 10:30–12:00, 13:00–16:30 Wed–Sun.

Religious Buildings

Religious Buildings
Auckland Cathedral of the Holy Trinity

Because of its relative youth, Auckland lacks the ancient churches and cathedrals of Europe, but this cathedral can claim to be the world's newest. A complex joining St Mary's Church, built in 1886, with a large contemporary building, the cathedral is a unique blend of Gothic and Pacific architecture. A centre for the performing arts as well as a place of worship, the cathedral is notable for its striking stained-glass window, while the new nave, with its expanse of forecourt, is evocative of a Polynesian meeting house. The cathedral is within easy walking distance of the Domain, Museum, Parnell Village, Ewelme Cottage and Kinder House.
✉ 446 Parnell Road,
☎ (09) 302 7203,
📠 (09) 302 7215,
⏲ 10:00–16:00 Mon–Sat, 13:00–17:00 Sun,
🚌 daily guided tours 11:30 and 14:30.

Art Galleries
The Auckland Art Gallery

The two public art galleries in the central city are Auckland Art Gallery Toi O Tamaki – the main gallery – and its contemporary art annexe, the New Gallery. The main gallery opened in 1887 and is a fine example of French Chateau-style architecture. It holds the most extensive collection of New Zealand and European artworks in the country, a total of 12,000 paintings. Classic works by Old Master 17th-century painters

---

Howick Historical Village

This living museum is a reconstruction of a Victorian colonial settlement in which visitor participation is encouraged. It preserves the early fencible settlement of Auckland during the 1840–80 period, when the fencible soldiers arrived in New Zealand. A fencible was a soldier liable for home service only.
✉ Bells Road, Lloyd Elsmore Park, Pakuranga
☎ (09) 576 9506
💻 www.fencible.org.nz

Below: *The Auckland Cathedral of the Holy Trinity in Parnell, which combines St Mary's Church (1886) with a new Nave, thus blending the best of colonial and contemporary Auckland architecture.*

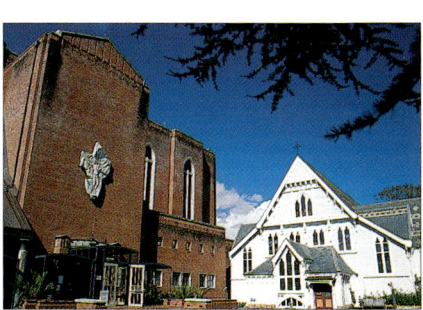

SIGHTSEEING

> **Colin McCahon – New Zealand's Greatest Painter**
>
> Colin McCahon (1919–87) is considered New Zealand's greatest painter and one who has achieved international acclaim. A slim, retiring man, he was raised in the South Island where he was influenced by cubism, modernism and the New Zealand landscape. In 1953 he moved with his wife and family to Auckland, where he spent the rest of his life, teaching at Elam Art School and influencing many younger painters. McCahon's paintings were often reviled during his lifetime by those who found his abstract style and religious themes enigmatic, but his reputation has grown steadily since his death, and today his works fetch hundreds of thousands of dollars. The Auckland City Art Gallery holds about 200 of McCahon's paintings, several of which are always on display.

and Victorian portrait artists Charles Goldie (1870–1947) and Gottfried Lindauer (1839–1926), through to works by contemporary New Zealand artists such as Ralph Hotere, Gretchen Albrecht and Bronwynne Cornish make the gallery a superb showcase. It regularly exhibits art works from international touring exhibitions.
✉ *corner of Wellesley and Kitchener Streets, southeast corner of Albert Park,*
☎ *24 hour Infoline (09) 379 1349,*
☎ *(09) 307 7700,*
📠 *(09) 302 1096,*
💻 *www.aucklandcity.govt.nz/artgallery*
✉ *gallery@akcity.govt.nz*
🕐 *10:00–17:00 daily,*
🚌 *free tours at 14:00 daily,*
💰 *ground floor of main gallery is free, charges ($12–$15) for special exhibitions held regularly, children 12 and under free,*
🍴 *shop and café within gallery.*

The New Gallery

The contemporary wing of the Auckland Art Gallery, the New Gallery opened in 1995 and presents changing and new exhibitions and artists' installations.
✉ *corner of Lorne and Wellesley Streets (directly across Kitchener Street from the main gallery),*
🕐 *10:00–17:00 daily,*
💰 *$4 adult, children 12 and under free,*
🍴 *New Gallery Café.*

Right: *The Auckland Art Gallery (1887), built in French Chateau-style architecture, corner Wellesley and Kitchener Streets.*

SPORT AND RECREATION

ACTIVITIES
Sport and Recreation

Auckland is sports-mad. A mild climate and the proximity of very long coastlines mean that almost every variety of summer and winter sport thrives in Auckland, attracting thousands of spectators and participants. Sporting events are some of the most keenly anticipated on the Auckland events calendar. Traditional New Zealand sports such as rugby, cricket, tennis and netball still lead the popularity stakes, but they are joined by water sports like sailing, swimming, rowing, kayaking, surfing, windsurfing and water polo, and individual competitions such as cycling, triathlons and marathons, as well as badminton, golf, lawn bowls, soccer, softball, squash, hockey and volleyball. Horse-racing is very popular, with day race meetings at Ellerslie and Avondale race courses and harness racing at Alexandra Park, Epsom.

Above: *Yachts racing on the Waitemata Harbour.*

Boating

Auckland is known as 'The City of Sails' for good reason. Sailing is a passion among many Aucklanders, young and old, while there are almost as many launches as yachts. The main venue for boating is the sheltered Waitemata Harbour, which opens out onto the Rangitoto Channel, the Tamaki Strait and the Hauraki Gulf. On these waters, boats of all shapes and sizes can be seen throughout the year, but especially in the warmer months from December through to April.

Westhaven Marina

The largest marina in the Southern Hemisphere, Westhaven Marina is one of Auckland's most distinctive marine features. Located in the lee of the harbour bridge at its southern end, the marina can accommodate nearly 2000 vessels. Around the long rows of pontoons and berths is a range of marine-related facilities, including chandleries, repair and refit services, 24-hour sewage pumpout, fresh water and power, and a large parking area. There are four yacht clubs beside the marina and a six-lane launch ramp. Maintenance facilities are near Westhaven Drive.
🖥 www.westhaven.co.nz

Activities

Surfing
The turbulent surf of the west coast is both a Mecca and a challenge for board-riders. An offshore northerly or easterly wind provides optimum conditions, smoothing out the Tasman Sea but not removing its large swells. Favourite spots are Maori Bay (Muriwai), Karekare and most sections of the coast at Piha. Further afield, Pakiri, Omaha and the Tawharanui Peninsula, near Warkworth, throw up fine waves when the wind turns easterly. These conditions also produce good surf at Orewa, Long Bay and Takapuna. Medlands, on Great Barrier Island's east coast, is a beautiful and highly regarded board-riding beach.

Swimming

Auckland is blessed with many fine swimming beaches. From the turbulent surf of the west coast to the gently lapping waters of the inner harbours, there are scores of places for keen sea swimmers to indulge themselves from December to April.

The black sand west coast beaches – like Karekare, Piha, Te Henga (Bethells) and Muriwai – experience turbulent surf, as the waves are driven by prevailing westerly and southwesterly winds from the Tasman Sea. Swimming here has been compared to being tossed about inside a washing machine. Rips – powerful outgoing currents – can also trap the unwary with potentially fatal results. It is therefore essential to swim only in the areas patrolled by lifeguards, i.e. between red and yellow flags planted in the sand.

On the eastern coast, by contrast, swimming is safe almost everywhere, though there can be light surf at the larger, more exposed northern beaches like Orewa, Long Bay and Takapuna. On the North Shore all the East Coast Bays beaches are lovely, in particular Castor Bay, Milford, Narrow Neck and Cheltenham, while on the city side of the harbour, Mission Bay, Bucklands Beach, St Heliers and Eastern Beach are all clean, safe and sheltered.

Rugby

Although not the dominating sporting and social force that it is in the rural areas of New Zealand, rugby union and

FUN FOR CHILDREN

rugby league are still played and followed by hundreds of thousands of Aucklanders. The season extends from late March to October, and every school and suburb has its rugby grounds. Schoolboy rugby is very competitive, with Saturday morning games and inter-school matches followed ardently. Headquarters for rugby union are Eden Park, in Sandringham, and the North Harbour Stadium at Albany on the North Shore. Major rugby league games are played at Ericsson Stadium, in Penrose.

Tennis

Though inter-club tennis is played throughout the Auckland region, the most anticipated tennis events are the international tournaments played every January: the ASB Classic Tennis premier women's competition and the Heineken Open men's tournament. The venue for both tournaments is the world-class ASB Tennis Centre in The Strand, Parnell. For two weeks in the New Year, this centre takes on the atmosphere of Wimbledon-down-under as world-ranked players compete for substantial monetary prizes, watched by sell-out crowds.

Fun for Children

There are scores of amusements for young people in Auckland.

Beaches

Swimming, surfing and boogie-boarding are good at west coast beaches like Karekare, Piha and Muriwai, or swim at peaceful east coast beaches like Long Bay, Takapuna and Cheltenham and the eastern suburbs ones – Mission Bay, Kohimarama and St Heliers.

Eden Park
Eden Park is the home of Auckland rugby and cricket. A sports ground since 1900, it became the headquarters for Auckland cricket in 1910 and rugby in 1925. Highlights in the park's history were the first cricket international between Auckland and Australia (1914), the first rugby international between New Zealand and South Africa (1921), the fourth test and first series win by the All Blacks over the Springboks (1956) and the first test victory by a New Zealand cricket team (over the West Indies) in 1957. The 1950 British Empire Games were held at Eden Park, as was the final of the inaugural Rugby World Cup competition, which the All Blacks won in 1987. Now a modern sporting complex complete with floodlights, corporate suites and conference facilities, Eden Park has a total crowd capacity of 45,000.
🖥 www.edenpark.co.nz

Opposite: *The distinctive All Black shirt and scarf both have the silver fern symbol.*

Activities

Public Pools
Parnell Seawater Baths
✉ Judges Bay, Parnell
☎ (09) 373 3561
⊕ 06:00–20:00 weekdays, 08:00–20:00 weekends

Philips Aquatic Centre
✉ Alberton Avenue, Mount Albert
☎ (09) 815 7005
💻 www.philipsaquatic.co.nz
⊕ 06:00–20:00 Mon–Thu, 06:00–21:00 Fri, 07:00–21:00 weekends

West Wave Aquatic Centre
✉ 19 Alderman Drive, Henderson
☎ (09) 836 8066
⊕ 09:00–20:00, daily

Tepid Baths
✉ 100 Customs Street
☎ (09) 379 4745
⊕ 06:00–20:45 weekdays, 07:00–19:00 weekends

Waiwera Infinity Thermal Spa Resort
✉ 7–11 Waiwera Road, Waiwera
☎ (Hibiscus Coast)
(09) 426 5369
💻 www.waiwera.co.nz
⊕ 09:00–22:00, daily

Palm Springs Thermal Pools
✉ 155 Parkhurst Road, Parakai
☎ (Helensville)
(09) 420 8321
⊕ 10:00–22:00 Sun–Thu, 10:00–00:00 Fri–Sat

Harbour Cruises
Cruise the Waitemata Harbour and Hauraki Gulf and visit the islands of the gulf.
Fullers Cruise Centre
✉ *Ferry Building, Quay Street,*
☎ *(09) 367 9102,*
💻 *www.fullers.co.nz*

Dolphin and Whale Watching
Watch from a boat especially designed for the purpose.
☎ *0800 220 111,*
💻 *www.dolphinplanet.co.nz*

Sea Kayaking
Try sea kayaking off Waiheke Island.
☎ *(09) 372 5550,*
💻 *www.kayakwaiheke.co.nz*

Regional Parks
Wenderholm, Long Bay, Omana and the Hunua Ranges have entertainment areas. *See page 25.*

Hiking
Hike the Waitakere Ranges, climb volcanic cones or go to the top of Rangitoto Island.

Auckland Harbour Bridge Climb
For great views.
✉ *Westhaven Reserve, Curran Street,*
☎ *0800 462 54 62,*
⊕ *10:00–19:00 daily,*
💻 *www.aucklandbridgeclimb.co.nz*

Rainbow's End Theme Park
Twenty-three acres of entertainment.
✉ *corner Great South and Wiri Station Roads, Manukau City, south Auckland,*
☎ *(09) 262 2044,*
⊕ *10:00–17:00 daily,*
💻 *www.rainbowsend.co.nz*

Victoria Park Market
Heaps of shops, stalls, arts, crafts and cafés.
✉ *210 Victoria Street West,* ☎ *(09) 309 6911*
⊕ *09:00–18:00 daily,*
💻 *www.victoria-park-market.co.nz*

Bungy Sky Screamer
✉ *corner Albert and Victoria Streets,*
☎ *(09) 377 1328,*
⊕ *11:00–22:00.*

CITY WALKS

City Walks

Walking (and jogging) are favourite pastimes for many Aucklanders. Popular places for walking include the slopes of volcanic cones such as Mount Eden Domain, One Tree Hill Domain, Mount Hobson and Mount St John on the city side, and North Head in Devonport. Other enjoyable walks include Tamaki Drive on the Waitemata waterfront, beaches such as Mission Bay, Kohimarama, St Heliers, Cheltenham and Takapuna, and the extensive grounds of the Auckland Domain. Further afield, the Waitakere Ranges are crisscrossed with bush hiking tracks, and the Coast to Coast walk takes hikers right across the Tamaki Isthmus, from the Waitemata to the Manukau Harbour.

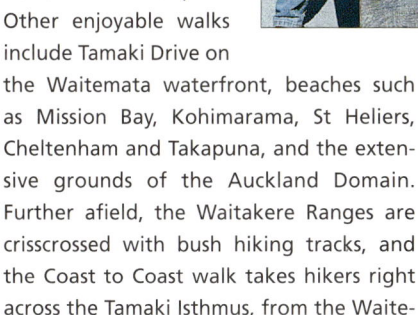

Above: *A pair of Maori youngsters proudly display their skateboards.*

The Coast to Coast Walk

The **Tamaki Isthmus**, New Zealand's narrowest neck of land, is never more than 9km (5.5 miles) wide. Walking across it, you cross from an inlet of the Pacific Ocean to one of the Tasman Sea. The Coast to Coast Walkway, taken in either direction, enables walkers to see some of the best natural and cultural features of central Auckland.

If starting at the **Viaduct Harbour** (Map B–D1), follow the yellow markers to Onehunga. If starting at **Onehunga** (Map B–E3), follow the blue markers to the Viaduct Harbour. The 16km (10-mile) walk

---

More Options for Children
Auckland Zoo (see page 23), Kelly Tarlton's Antarctic Encounter and Underwater World (see page 17), the Sky Tower (see page 16), the Auckland Museum (see page 14), the National Maritime Museum (see page 20), the Museum of Transport and Technology (see page 22), Cinemas (see page 73), the Viaduct Harbour (see page 15).
Good websites are:
🖥 www.aucklandtourism.co.nz
🖥 www.kidsauckland.com

ACTIVITIES

Above: Pond and gardens in the Auckland Domain.

takes 4–6 hours at an easy walking pace, and buses run in both directions to return walkers to their starting point. Following the walk from north to south, it begins at the Viaduct Harbour and includes Princes Street, the Domain, Mountain Road, Mount Eden Domain, Melville Park, One Tree Hill Domain and Manukau Road, before ending at the Onehunga Bay Reserve, at the Manukau Harbour. Pamphlets are available from Auckland's Information Centres.

A Central City Walk

Begin in **Vulcan Lane** (Map A–D2), four streets up from the bottom of Queen Street. Turn right off this pedestrian-only lane, with its cafés and bars, and into High Street, one of the city's most appealing streets. Walk across Freyberg Place and Courthouse Lane into the Chancery precinct, where many leading fashion boutiques are located. Go through the Chancery, up the steps and cross Kitchener Street into the northern extension of Albert Park, then up Bowen Avenue to the intersection with Princes Street. Across the intersection, on the corner of Waterloo Quadrant, is a colonial gatehouse. Walk down the drive and through the lovely grounds to Old Government House (1856), one-time residence of the Governors of New Zealand and now the University of Auckland's Senior Common Room. In the centre of the university campus are the remnants of the walls of a military barracks,

---

Devonport to Takapuna Walk

At low tide only, a peaceful beach walk can be taken from Devonport to Takapuna, in either direction. The walk takes about one and a half hours, and is mostly on sand, with some rocks to be climbed over at the headlands. From Devonport the walk starts at the northern end of Cheltenham Beach and includes Narrow Neck Beach, a long stretch of sand and rocks at the base of high cliffs below Seacliffe Avenue, then past St Leonards Beach to Takapuna Beach.

CITY WALKS

built in the 1840s. Emerge from the university grounds at the Clock Tower and cross back over Princes Street to Albert Park. Walk across the park and down the steps to Kitchener Street, then turn left past the Auckland Art Gallery to Wellesley Street. Turn right, down to Queen Street. On the corner of Wellesley and Queen Streets is the Civic theatre (see page 72). Further up Queen Street is Aotea Square and The Edge (💻 www.the-edge.co.nz), a modern complex containing the Aotea Centre (see page 72) and the Force Entertainment Centre.

Takapuna to Milford Walk

The coastline between the Takapuna Beach boat ramp and Black Rock, Milford, is one of great geological and historical interest. *The Takapuna–Milford Walk*, another heritage trail publication brought out by the North Shore City Council (and obtainable from Information Centres), incorporates many natural and cultural features found in this area. The walk begins by the ancient pohutukawa trees at the northern end of Takapuna Beach (Map C–E4) and passes the Old Post Office and Telephone Exchange at 187a Hurstmere Road. A path along the rocks just past O'Neills Avenue takes the walker past the Fossil Forest where the imprints of trees, engulfed by lava from the crater of what is now Lake Pupuke about 100,000 years ago, can still be seen. At low tide about 500 tree stump moulds can be seen on the reef by the Takapuna Boat Ramp. Other features of the walk are the oak trees growing from Minnehaha Avenue and O'Neills Avenue, Algie's Castle, Thorne Bay and the lava landform that is Black Rock.

Takapuna Literary Walks

The Takapuna–Milford district, like Devonport, has been home to many of New Zealand's best-known poets, playwrights, short-story writers and novelists. Pioneer writer and mentor to many of these literary figures was Frank Sargeson (1903–82), whose cottage, at 14 Esmonde Road, Takapuna, is preserved as a literary museum. The writer lived and wrote here for over 50 years. The key to the Sargeson House can be borrowed from the Takapuna Public Library, the Promenade, Takapuna. A North Shore City publication, *North Shore Literary Walks*, provides details of the life of Frank Sargeson and the other distinguished New Zealand writers who have lived and worked on the North Shore. The North Shore heritage trail booklets published by North Shore City, including a Browns Bay Walk, can be obtained from the Visitor Centres in Devonport and Takapuna. Also refer to 💻 www.northshorecity.govt.nz

ACTIVITIES

> **Bastion Point Walk**
> Start at the Selwyn Domain, in Mission Bay. Walk towards the city, along Tamaki Drive on the waterfront as far as Hapimana Street. Follow this street up to the Michael Joseph Savage Memorial, with its sunken gardens and cliff-top views of the Waitemata Harbour. Take the walking track back down the hill to Mission Bay.

Below: *The Michael Joseph Savage Memorial on Bastion Point commemorates New Zealand's much-loved Prime Minister of the 1930s.*

Organized Tours
ABC Tours
Morning and afternoon city tours. The morning tour takes in Westhaven marina, Ponsonby, Mt Eden, the Auckland Museum and eastern suburbs. The afternoon tour goes coast to coast: Devonport, Takapuna, the east coast beaches, then west Auckland.
☎ *0800 222 868,*
✆ *(09) 849 6644,*
🖥 *www.abctours.co.nz*

Auckland Explorer
'Hop on, Hop off' bus, with commentary on Auckland's top 14 attractions.
✉ *departs from Ferry Building, Quay Street,*
☎ *0800 439 756,*
⏱ *every 30 minutes from 09:00, hourly from 10:00 in winter,*
🖥 *www.explorerbus.co.nz*

Cruising Auckland
Two-hour, half-day and day tours of the Waitemata Harbour, Hauraki Gulf and its islands (Rangitoto, Tiritiri Matangi, Waiheke).
Fullers Cruise Centre,
✉ *Ferry Building, Quay Street,*
☎ *(09) 367 9111,*
🖥 *www.fullers.co.nz*

Ferry Trips
Waitemata Harbour, and to Kawau Island and Coromandel town.
✉ *Pier 3, Quay Street,*
☎ *0800 888 006,*
🖥 *www.kawaukat.co.nz*

Scenic Tours New Zealand
Auckland Highlights Half Day Tours. A three-hour tour with commentary in an air-conditioned coach
☎ *0800 698 687,*
🖥 *www.scenictours.co.nz*

Bush and Beach
Full or half-day guided eco-tours of Auckland's rainforests and black sand beaches.
☎ *(09) 837 4193,*
✆ *(09) 837 4193*
🖥 *www.bushandbeach.co.nz*

ORGANIZED TOURS

Wine Tasting Tours
Small group tours of the region's vineyards.
☎ (09) 630 1540,
💻 www.winetrailtours co.nz

Fly Warbirds Dakota
A scenic flight over Auckland in a genuine World War II DC3.
☎ (09) 479 1378,
💻 www.nzwarbirds.org.nz
✉ flydc3@paradise.net.nz

Bay of Islands
1–3 days, including Cape Reinga and swimming with dolphins.
✉ Bay of Islands Travel Centre, Customs Street,
☎ (09) 358 0259,
📠 (09) 302 1444,
💻 www.boitc.co.nz

New Zealand Sightseeing
Daily tours of Auckland, Bay of Islands, Waitomo and Rotorua, by luxury coach, departing from the Sightseeing Centre.
✉ 180 Quay Street,
☎ 0800 744 487,
💻 www.greatsights.co.nz

Kea Campers (NZ) Ltd
Fully equipped campervans and motorhomes for hire.
☎ 0800 52 00 52
💻 www.keacampers.com

Tour Masters
Flexible package tours. Options for the North and South Islands; specials to Rotorua and the Bay of Islands.
☎ 0800 80 3550.

Coromandel Peninsula
Day tours visiting the old gold-mining town of Thames, then crossing the mountains to the east coast beaches.
✉ Interland Tours, PO Box 479, Auckland,
☎ (09) 524 8556,
🕗 depart 08:30, return 18:30; hotel and motel pick-up & drop-off available.

A City Cycling Tour
The Waitemata waterfront and Tamaki Drive feature prominently on Auckland's 50km (30-mile) Cycle Route, which can be followed clockwise or anticlockwise. Cycling clockwise and starting at One Tree Hill, the route passes through the suburbs of Mount Eden, Mount Albert, Westmere, St Marys Bay and Parnell, before descending to the southern waterfront by the Parnell Seawater Baths. At the eastern end of the circuit, Achilles Point, the route turns inland and traces the western side of the Tamaki estuary. Points of interest along the circuit include the Auckland Museum, the Museum of Transport and Technology, the Zoo and Point Erin Baths. Detailed maps of the route are available from Auckland's Information Centres. NB In New Zealand it is compulsory for cyclists to wear safety helmets at all times.

SHOPPING

Above: *The shopping centre at Titirangi Village, west Auckland.*

Lively High Street
This narrow street, which runs parallel to Queen Street on its eastern side, has personality aplenty. Packed with bookshops, bars, florists, giftshops, cafés and fashion boutiques, High Street is lively and convivial at any time of the day, but particularly at night, when some of the bars, notably **Deschlers**, provide live jazz. **Unity Books**, right next to Deschlers, is the favoured bookshop of Auckland's literary community. Crossing High Street is the pedestrian-only and very stylish **Vulcan Lane**, noted for its bars, cafés, coffee bars and fashionwear shops.

Shops

There is shopping to suit all pockets throughout Auckland, from the suburban mega-malls to the street markets of Otara and Avondale and the stylish boutiques of Ponsonby and Parnell. The best shopping in and around the central business district is behind Queen Street.

Queen Street

Although the city's central thoroughfare, Queen Street is not rated the top shopping street. However, the flagship shop of the **Whitcoulls** books chain is on the Victoria Street corner, and there are some quality boutiques in Queens and Victoria arcades, while **Smith & Caughey** (✉ 253–261 Queen Street) upholds its position as Auckland's most venerable department store. There are some very good jewellery shops at the lower end of Queen Street, including **Marshall's Opals and Fine Gold Jewellery**,
✉ *93 Queen Street.*

Real Groovy

A huge selection of clothes, magazines, books, and contemporary music.
✉ *438 Queen Street.*

Downtown Block

This block has three enclosed levels of mainly clothing, gift and souvenir shops, as well as a Post Shop, pharmacy, food hall, a Whitcoulls bookshop and a Warehouse.
✉ *The foot of Queen Street, next to Queen Elizabeth II Square.*

DFS Galleria

The city's largest duty-free emporium is housed in this historic Customs House.
✉ *Across from Downtown, on the corner of Customs and Albert Streets.*

Regency Duty Free

A good duty-free shop.
✉ *25 Victoria Street West.*

SHOPS

Auckland International Airport

Has a comprehensive range of excellent duty-free shops.
☎ Airport Infoline 0800 247 767,
🖥 www.airportshoppers.com

Chancery Precinct

Specializes in upmarket apparel shops. Many of the country's top fashion designers are represented, including Feline, Tanya Carlson, Karen Walker, Morrison Hotel and Zambesi.
✉ Just across Freyberg Place from High Street.

The Story Box

Hand-crafted gifts, crafts and art.
✉ Shop 46 Bacons Lane, the Chancery.

Atrium on Elliot

A three-level quality retail complex of fashion shops and ethnic restaurants.
✉ Elliot Street, one back from Queen Street behind Smith & Caughey.

Karangahape Road

Crossing the top of Queen Street is **Karangahape Road**, ('K-Road'). This colourful street is an eclectic, multicultural blend of coffee bars, pubs, food stores, restaurants and bars, morphing at its western end into nightclubs, strip clubs and massage parlours. 'K-Road' also holds a **'Trash and Treasures' market** ✉ 'K-Road' carpark, ⏰ 06:00–11:00, Sundays.

Beyond the Central City

Ponsonby Road and **Parnell Road** are considered at the top end of Auckland's retail districts, as is **Broadway**, Newmarket's main street. Close to Broadway is Auckland's most affluent suburb, **Remuera**, whose main street is lined with quality shops offering goods of all kinds.

North Shore

The main streets of Devonport, Takapuna

Antique Shops

Auckland's early settlers were mainly from the working classes, so they did not have valuable antiques to bring with them to the new settlement. However, as the town and its citizens prospered, the early Aucklanders imported quality furniture, glass, porcelain and jewellery from Britain and Europe, to match their improved status. Today, some of these items can be found in the city's antique shops, and many of these shops are grouped, making browsing and shopping easier. For example, there is a group of antique shops at the corner of Great South Road and Market Road, near Greenlane, and another not far away at the intersection of Greenlane and Manukau Roads, in Epsom. The older, affluent suburbs of Devonport, Parnell and Remuera also have several antique dealers in their shopping areas. The Yellow Pages of the Auckland telephone directory lists more than a hundred antique dealers, though bric-a-brac shops would be a more apt description for many of these. But there is still always the possibility that a real treasure will be discovered, even here.

SHOPPING

Top Bookshops
Unity Books
✉ 19 High Street, central city
Parsons Bookshop
✉ New Gallery Building, corner Lorne and Wellesley Streets
Time Out Bookstore
✉ 432 Mount Eden Road, Mount Eden
Paradox Books
✉ 26 Victoria Road, Devonport
Borders Books & Music
✉ 291–297 Queen Street, central city
The Booklover
✉ 67 Hurstmere Road, Takapuna
Wheelers Bookshop
✉ 395 Remuera Road, Remuera
Wild Swans Bookstore
✉ 134 Kitchener Road, Milford
Women's Bookshop
✉ 105 Ponsonby Road, Ponsonby

Second-hand Bookshops
Dead Poets Bookstore
✉ 238 Karangahape Road-George Court
Hard to Find (but worth the effort)
✉ 171–173 The Mall, Onehunga, and 81A Victoria Road, Devonport
Rare Books
✉ 6 High Street, central city
Evergreen Books
✉ 15 Victoria Road, Devonport
Bookmark Secondhand Books
✉ Parkway Arcade, 46–54 Hurstmere Road, Takapuna

and Mairangi Bay have a good range of shops and a relaxed, seaside atmosphere to shop in. Takapuna and Mairangi Bay specialize in apparel shops, while there are two excellent second-hand bookshops in Devonport, **Hard to Find** and **Evergreen**.

The Suburbs

There are large shopping malls at Takapuna, Glenfield and Albany, on the North Shore and at Westgate in Massey, West City at Henderson, Botany Downs, near Howick and Manukau City in south Auckland. **Westfield St Lukes**, Mount Albert, is considered one of the city's top shopping malls.

Dress-Smart Factory Outlet Centre

Over 60 factory stores retailing everything from fashion to homeware at reduced prices.
✉ *151 Arthur Street, Onehunga,* 🖥 *www.dress-smart.co.nz*

Bookshops

Auckland has many excellent bookshops, including several quality second-hand stores. Branches of the **Whitcoulls** chain are widespread and there are also three **Dymocks** branches. Independent shops offer knowledgeable service. *See* side panel.

Markets

Some of the liveliest buying and selling in Auckland occurs at the city's street markets. They offer goods at bargain prices, and stall-holders are sometimes open to reasonable offers lower than the marked price. As usual with markets, customers can't be too early, as all get under way not long after daybreak.

Otara Fleamarket

Largest and most distinctively South Pacific of the markets, **Otara Fleamarket** is situated in a predominantly Maori and Pacific Island neighbourhood.

MARKETS

The food stalls offer Pacific Island, Indian, Chinese and European fruit, vegetables and seafood, and takeaways from chop suey to doughnuts. There are also Pacific fabrics, Polynesian artefacts, clothing, jewellery, footwear and second-hand goods. Adding to the Pacific Island ambience is the local music: hip-hop, reggae, ukeleles and guitars. It's easy to spend a whole morning at Otara's vibrant, multicultural market.
✉ *Newbury Sreet, (off Southern Motorway),*
🕒 *Saturdays.*

Victoria Park Market

A maze of 85 shops, stalls, bars and eateries, within a brick-walled enclosure.
✉ *210 Victoria Street West,* ☎ *(09) 309 6911,* 💻 *www.victoria-park-market.co.nz,*
🕒 *09:00–18:00 daily.*

Takapuna Market

Takapuna's market offers everything from second-hand tools and books to plants, shellfish, vegetables and picture frames.
✉ *Main carpark alongside Lake Road,*
🕒 *Sunday mornings.*

Aotea Square Market

Here stall-holders sell their wares from small, colourful tents, and the otherwise dull square is enlivened further by musical performances. On offer is a range of foods, local arts and crafts and clothing. This market is more upmarket than the others. Its vegetables, for example, are mainly organic, and many of the clothes have designer labels.
✉ *Aotea Square, just off Queen Street, near the centre of the city,*
🕒 *10:00–18:00, Friday and Saturday.*

La Cigale

A French-style, farmers market.
✉ *69 St Georges Bay Road, Parnell,*
🕒 *08:00–13:00, every Saturday.*

Above: *Souvenir T-shirts at Otara Market.*

Auckland Fish Market

New market complex featuring ocean-fresh fish, meats, fruit and vegetables, delicatessen goods, cafés and seafood school. Free shuttle bus from central city, or a 15-minute walk west of the Information Centre at Viaduct Harbour.
✉ between Jellicoe and Madden Streets, Freemans Bay
☎ (09) 379 1490
💻 www.afm.co.nz
🕒 07:00–19:00, daily

ACCOMMODATION

Right: *The Hilton Hotel, on Princes Wharf, has views of the Waitemata Harbour from every room.*

WHERE TO STAY

There is a wide range of accommodation available in and around Auckland, from five-star hotels to self-catering apartments and motels. Most of the top quality hotels are near the central business district or the waterfront, where there are also apartments. New Zealand motels are almost always self-catering, with full cooking facilities on the premises, and this type of accommodation is found more commonly in the city's suburbs. There are also several budget hotels and backpacker hostels quite close to the central city. Hotel and motel chains can be accessed through listings in the Auckland Yellow Pages, 💻 www.yellowpages.co.nz

The accommodation here has been grouped into three areas: **Central City**, **North Shore** and **Outer Auckland**, then into categories. All the North Shore accommodation listed is within easy reach of either the motorway and the harbour bridge or the Devonport ferry. In the Outer Auckland category, all accommodation is under an hour's drive or ferry trip from Downtown Auckland.

Great Barrier Island
(Map D–F2)
For those seeking escape from the pressures of city life, Great Barrier, the largest island in the Hauraki Gulf, is ideal. It offers fine beaches, bush walks and an unhurried way of life.

Oasis Lodge
Secluded natural surroundings and tranquillity on the Hauraki Gulf's largest island. Deluxe accommodation, international cuisine and a vineyard producing the lodge's own Cabernet Sauvignon.
✉ Tryphena RD1, Great Barrier Island
☎ (09) 429 0021
📠 (09) 429 0034
💻 www.barrieroasis.net
✉ enquiries@barrieroasis.co.nz

WHERE TO STAY

Central City
• *LUXURY HOTELS*

Hilton Auckland
(Map A–D1)
This newish hotel is located at the end of Princes Wharf, giving grandstand views of all the waterfront's nautical activities. It's also only a stroll away from Downtown Auckland and the Britomart Centre. All rooms have private balconies.
☎ (09) 978 2000,
📠 (09) 978 2001,
💻 www.hilton.com

Rendezvous Auckland
(Map A–C3)
Located in the heart of the entertainment area, with an underpass to Aotea Square. Five-star rooms, plus a gymnasium, sauna and indoor heated pool.
✉ corner Mayoral Drive and Vincent Street,
☎ (09) 366 3000,
📠 (09) 366 0121,
💻 www.rendezvous auckland.com
✍ res@carlton-auckland.co.nz

Hyatt Regency Auckland
(Map A–E2)
A recent $65m expansion has added 132 one- and two-bedroom apartments to the existing 274 rooms. The Hyatt's elevated position provides panoramic views over the Waitemata Harbour and Albert Park.
✉ corner Waterloo Quadrant & Princes Street,
☎ (09) 355 1234,
📠 (09) 302 3269,
💻 www.aucklandhyatt.com
✍ auckland@hyatt.co.nz

Stamford Plaza
(Map A–D2)
A convenient downtown location and five-star rating make this a highly recommended hotel. Located a short walk away from the Viaduct Harbour, this hotel has just undergone a complete refurbishment.
✉ lower Albert Street,
☎ (09) 309 8888,
📠 (09) 379 6445,
💻 www.stamford.com.au
✍ reservations@spak.stamford.com.au

The Ascott Metropolis Auckland
(Map A–D2)
One- and two-bedroom, self-contained suites in a quiet setting adjacent to Albert Park and quality shopping precincts.
✉ Number 1 Courthouse Lane,
☎ (09) 300 8800,
📠 (09) 300 8899,
💻 www.the-ascott.com
✍ enquiry.auckland@the-ascott.com

Langham Hotel Auckland
(Map A–D3)
Award-winning hotel with luxuriously appointed rooms and Health Club, located near the top end of Queen Street.
✉ 83 Symonds Street,
☎ (09) 379 5132,
📠 (09) 377 4075,
💻 www.langhamhotels.com
✍ akl.resrv@langhamhotels.com

ACCOMMODATION

Mercure Hotel Windsor Auckland (Map A–D2)
A refurbished heritage building in the heart of the retail district. Most guest rooms have kitchenettes.
✉ *58–60 Queen Street, central Auckland,*
☎ *(09) 309 9979,*
🖥 *www.accorhotels.co.nz*

• CITY APARTMENTS
Latitude 37 Apartments (Map A–C2)
Serviced studio, one-, two- and three-bedroom apartments right beside the Viaduct Harbour and only minutes away from Downtown. Basement parking included.
✉ *22 Pakenham St East, Viaduct Harbour,*
☎ *0800 452 848,*
✆ *(09) 309 7850,*
🖥 *www.latitude37.co.nz*
✉ *info@latitude37.co.nz*

The Railway Campus (Map A–F2)
Modern one-, two- and three-bedroom, self-catering apartments in a refurbished heritage building. 1km (0.6 miles) to the CBD.
✉ *26–48 Te Taou Crescent, near Parnell,*
☎ *(09) 367 7100,*
✆ *(09) 367 7101,*
🖥 *www.auckland.ac.nz/accommodation*
✉ *railcamp@auckland.ac.nz*

Cintra Lane Serviced Apartment/Hotel (Map A–D3)
Studio and one-bedroom apartments with fully equipped kitchen. Nightly/weekly rates.
✉ *3 Whitaker Place, central Auckland,*
☎ *(09) 379 6288,*
✆ *(09) 379 6277,*
res. 0800 246 872,
🖥 *www.questcintra.co.nz*
✉ *reception@cintra.co.nz*

SkyCity Grand Hotel (Map A–D3)
A five-star hotel close to Queen Street, with fitness centre and pool.
✉ *90 Federal Street, central Auckland,*
☎ *(09) 363 7000,*
🖥 *www.skycitygrand.co.nz*

• CITY MOTELS
Great South Road Motor Lodge (Map B–E2)
Studio and family units, all with cooking facilities. Garden setting, on major bus route.
✉ *112 Great South Road, Newmarket,*
☎ *(09) 520 5509,*
✆ *(09) 524 5718,*
🖥 *www.gsrmlodge.co.nz*

Abaco on Jervois (Map A–A1)
Self-catering apartments within easy walk of Herne Bay and Ponsonby shops and restaurants, and Victoria Park market.
✉ *59 Jervois Road, Ponsonby,*
☎ *(09) 376 0119,*
🖥 *www.abacospamotel.com*

• CITY BED AND BREAKFAST
Ascot Parnell (Map A–F3)
This small hotel is

56

WHERE TO STAY

located in a pleasant neighbourhood. Comfortable spacious *en-suite accommodation.*
✉ *36 St Stephens Avenue, Parnell,*
☎ *(09) 309 9012,*
📠 *(09) 309 3729,*
🖥 *www.ascotparnell.com*
✆ *ascotparnell@compuserve.com*

Bavaria Bed & Breakfast Hotel
(Map A–C6)
Small hotel in a quiet mature suburb, close to city bus routes. Rooms with *en suites.*
✉ *83 Valley Road, Mount Eden,*
☎ *(09) 638 9641,*
📠 *(09) 638 9665,*
🖥 *www.bavariabandbhotel.co.nz*

Aspen House Budget Bed and Breakfast
(Map A–E2)
Five minutes' walk to central city; twin/double rooms; shared *bathroom facilities.*
✉ *62 Emily Place, central Auckland,*
☎ *(09) 379 6633,*
📠 *(09) 379 6634,*
🖥 *www.aspenhouse.co.nz*
✆ *aspenhouse@xtra.co.nz*

• CITY BACKPACKERS
ACB Auckland Central Backpackers
(Map A–D2)
Modern facilities, close to all city amenities, internet *café/call centre.*
✉ *Level 3, 229 Queen Street,*
☎ *(09) 358 4877,*
📠 *(09) 358 4872,*
🖥 *www.acb.co.nz*
✆ *backpackers@acb.co.nz*

Auckland International YHA
(Map A–D3)
Close to upper Queen Street, modern facilities, private and *en-suite rooms available.*
✉ *18 Liverpool Street and 5 Turner Street, central Auckland,*
☎ *(09) 302 8200,*
📠 *(09) 302 8205,*
reservations 0800 278 299,
🖥 *www.yha.co.nz*
✆ *book@yha.org.nz*

North Shore
• LUXURY HOTELS
The Spencer on Byron
(Map C–E4)
A North Shore landmark, this high-rise 249-suite hotel situated in the heart of Takapuna on the North Shore has panoramic views of the Shore and Auckland City. It is within easy walking distance to the beach and shops, and a few minutes' drive to the Northern Motorway and *harbour bridge.*
✉ *9–17 Byron Avenue, Takapuna,*
☎ *(09) 916 6111, NZ toll free 0800 773 623,*
📠 *64-9-916-6110,*
🖥 *www.spencerbyron.co.nz*

The Esplanade Hotel
(Map C–E5)
Edwardian charm and elegance, right on the waterfront opposite the ferry terminal.

ACCOMMODATION

The Esplanade Hotel has beautifully refurbished rooms, with excellent views over Devonport and the inner Waitemata Harbour and a dignified dining room downstairs.
✉ corner Queens Parade and Victoria Road, Devonport,
☎ (09) 445 1291,
📠 (09) 445 1999,
💻 www.esplanadehotel.co.nz
✆ reservations@esplanadehotel.co.nz

- *MOTELS*

Parklane Motor Inn
(Map C–E4)
This establishment has modern units, close to Takapuna Beach and only a few minutes from the harbour bridge.
✉ corner Lake Road and Rewiti Avenue, Takapuna,
☎ (09) 486 1069,
📠 (09) 486 2658,
💻 www.parklane.co.nz
✆ accom@parklane.co.nz

Auckland North Shore Motels & Holiday Park
(Map C–D4)
Quiet setting handy to Northern Motorway and North Shore shops.
✉ 52 Northcote Road, Takapuna,
☎ (09) 418 2578,
📠 (09) 480 0435,
✆ info@nsmotels.co.nz

- *BED AND BREAKFAST*

Hampton Beach House
(Map C–F5)
This bed and breakfast is situated in a large, tastefully restored house right on the Devonport waterfront, just a stroll away from the local shops and cafés and with views over the Waitemata Harbour. Also features a courtyard and private garden.
✉ 4 King Edward Parade, Devonport,
☎ (09) 445 1358,
💻 www.hamptonbeachhouse.co.nz

Devonport Views Bed and Breakfast
(Map C–F5)
Garden rooms and a cottage in a 1920s home on a ridge above Devonport village, with views over Auckland Harbour. Three minutes' walk to the village and the ferry to the central city.
✉ 79 Calliope Road, Devonport,
☎ (09) 445 1118,
💻 www.devonportviews.co.nz

Outer Auckland

- *HOTEL*

Heritage Hotel Du Vin & Firstland Vineyards
(Map D–D6)
Chalet-style rooms, restaurant and leisure facilities, in vineyard setting, 45 minutes' drive south of the city.
✉ Lyons Road, Pokeno,
☎ (09) 233 6314,
📠 (09) 233 6215,
💻 www.heritagehotels.co.nz

Where to Stay

✆ reservations@duvin.co.nz

• **LUXURY LODGE**
Te Whau Lodge
(Map D–D5)
Secluded accommodation in a peaceful island setting, overlooking Putiki Bay and the Waitemata Harbour. It is ideal for couples or small groups.
✉ 36 Vintage Lane, Waiheke Island,
☎ (09) 372 2288,
📠 (09) 372 2218,
💻 www.tewhaulodge.co.nz
✆ lizandgene@tewhaulodge.co.nz

• **COTTAGE ACCOMMODATION**
A Chalet in the Ferns
(Map D–B5)
Self-contained, four-guest cottage surrounded by native forest and garden, 30 minutes' drive from central Auckland. A short walk from Titirangi's cafés and art galleries.
✉ 81 Park Road, Titirangi,
☎ (09) 817 1956,
💻 www.thefernschalet.co.nz

Bethells Beach Cottages
(Map D–A5)
Two cottages set among the west coast's spectacular scenery. Lake and sea swimming, coastal walks.
✉ Bethells Road, Bethells Beach, Te Henga, west coast,
☎ (09) 810 9581,
📠 (09) 810 8677,
💻 www.bethellsbeach.com
✆ info@bethellsbeach.com

Panorama Heights Bed and Breakfast
(Map D–A5)
Private, peaceful setting with expansive views over the kauri forest, east to Auckland city and beyond. A great outlook, by day or night.
✉ 42 Kitewaho Road, Swanson, west Auckland.
☎ (09) 832 4777,
💻 www.panoramaheights.com
✆ nzbnb4u@clear.net.nz

Piha Lodge
(Map D–A5)
Two self-contained units high above a popular west coast beach, with spectacular coast and bush views. Sunsets a speciality.
✉ 117 Piha Road,
☎ (09) 812 8595,
💻 www.pihalodge.co.nz
✆ pihalodge@xtra.co.nz

Rangiwai Lodge
(Map B–B3)
Luxury boutique lodge set among the bush with great harbour and forest views. Close to popular and pretty Titirangi village.
✉ 29 Rangiwai Road, Titirangi,
☎ (09) 817 8990,
💻 www.accommodation-nz.com
✆ rangiwai@ihug.co.nz

EATING OUT

Auckland's Wines
Favoured wines for Aucklanders are New Zealand whites, particularly the fresh, crisp Sauvignon Blancs, Chardonnays and Methode Champenoise sparkling wines. Favoured reds are the Hawkes Bay Cabernet Sauvignons and Martinborough and Central Otago Pinot Noirs, which, like the Marlborough-grown Sauvignon Blancs and Chardonnays, have achieved a world-wide reputation for quality and value. Most Aucklanders woke up to the fact some years ago that New Zealand sparkling wines were every bit as good and less than half the price of their French equivalents. Whether it's still or sparkling wine, it's unnecessary to pay more than $NZ20 for an excellent local vintage in liquor stores or supermarkets, though the listed price of wine in a non-BYO restaurant will be double the wholesale cost.

EATING OUT

Auckland offers an enormous variety of dining options, from restaurants of every ethnicity to fashionable waterfront cafés to hotel dining rooms whose menus feature innovative Pacific Rim cuisine. The food served is almost always fresh, as the sources of fish, meat and vegetables are close to the city. Many restaurants are **licensed**, meaning that they serve their own liquor, others offer Bring Your Own (BYO) as well as their own wine list. If you bring your own, you will be charged corkage of $2 upwards per bottle. It's advisable to book in advance at most restaurants, particularly on Fridays and Saturdays. **Tipping** of service staff is not obligatory, but can be offered in exchange for particularly considerate table service.

What to Eat
The choice of cuisine in Auckland is sometimes bewildering, as there is something to suit every style and every palate. Immigration from Asia in recent years has led to a proliferation of Chinese, Thai, Korean, Malaysian and Indian restaurants in particular, but there are also many Italian, Turkish and French eateries. Sushi bars are also found throughout Auckland. There are clusters of restaurants in and around the city, as well as individual establishments everywhere, with the Yellow Pages of the Auckland telephone directory containing no fewer than 23 pages of licensed and BYO restaurants.

WHERE TO EAT

Where to Eat

The main eating-out districts are located around the **Viaduct Harbour** and **Princes Wharf**, where there are literally rows of restaurants, and similarly at **Mission Bay**, on the eastern waterfront. **Parnell Road** has many excellent cafés and restaurants, while **Ponsonby Road** and nearby **Jervois Road** are definitely latte-land, but as well as coffee bars and cafés there are many restaurants in these two upmarket streets. There are also food halls near the bottom end of **Queen Street**, in the **Downtown** complex, in the **Force Entertainment Centre** in Queen Street and in **Broadway**, Newmarket, where tasty and reasonably priced snacks are obtainable at all hours of the day. On the North Shore, Devonport's main street, **Victoria Road**, has several eateries from the bottom of the street to the top. In Takapuna there are a number of restaurants in **Hurstmere Road**, both in the main shopping centre and through the other side at the Milford end, while in each of the East Coast Bays there is at least one quality restaurant.

Auckland's many **pubs** also provide lunch and evening meals. Although not haute cuisine, pub meals are cheaper than in a restaurant and the portions are usually generous, giving excellent value.

Above: *One of the many restaurants on Princes Wharf, near the Viaduct Harbour.*
Opposite: *High Street has several pavement cafés.*

Wining and Dining

Many of the Auckland region's vineyards combine wine tastings and sales with café dining. In the Kumeu, Henderson, Te Kauwhata and Matakana wine-making districts there are quality cafés attached to several wineries, enabling visitors to sample the best of local vegetables, meats, breads, cheeses and seafood, along with the area's Chardonnays, Rieslings and Sauvignon Blancs. Waiheke Island is another location where the café food and local wines complement each other superbly.

EATING OUT

Where to Eat

• LUXURY

Antoines
A Parnell and Auckland institution, this restaurant has set enviable standards of food and service for many years.
✉ 333 Parnell Road,
☎ (09) 379 8756.

Mikano
Right on the waterfront, with sea views across to Devonport, this superbly sited restaurant specializes in innovative cuisine, especially seafood.
✉ 1 Solent Street, Mechanics Bay,
☎ (09) 309 9514.

Rice
Striking modern décor and an international menu in which rice in its infinite manifestations features prominently.
✉ 10/12 Federal Street, central city,
☎ (09) 359 9113.

White
The unique location towards the end of the wharf allows absorbing views along with the maritime activities outside.
✉ Hilton Auckland, Princes Wharf,
☎ (09) 978 2020.

Vinnies
The premier restaurant on this popular dining row offers top cuisine and service in tasteful surroundings.
✉ 199 Jervois Road, Herne Bay,
☎ (09) 376 5597.

• MID-RANGE

Harbourside
Relaxed dining, with seafood a speciality, inside or on the balcony overlooking the waterfront.
✉ 1st Floor, Ferry Building, Quay Street,
☎ (09) 307 0556.

Orbit
This à la carte restaurant revolves 360° in an hour, giving matchless views of the entire city from its highest point.
✉ Sky Tower, corner Victoria & Federal Streets, central city,
☎ (09) 363 6000.

Prego
One of Auckland's longest-established restaurants, specializing in delicious pasta and pizza.
✉ 226 Ponsonby Road, Ponsonby,
☎ (09) 376 3095.

O'Connell Street Bistro
Very popular, particularly for lunches, with an intimate, European ambience.
✉ 3 O'Connell Street, central city,
☎ (09) 377 1884.

Number 5 Wine Bistro
Unpretentious and discreetly located, with high standards of food and a superior wine list.
✉ 5 City Road,
☎ (09) 309 9273.

Daikoku Japanese Steak House
Japanese cuisine, cooked at the diners' table. Near the waterfront. Also in Takapuna and Botany Downs.
✉ 148 Quay Street,
☎ (09) 302 2432.

WHERE TO EAT

Cin Cin on Quay Brasserie and Bar
Tasteful décor and a lovely setting beside the harbour.
✉ Ferry Building, 99 Quay Street,
☎ (09) 307 6966.

Andiamo Restaurant & Bar
Stylish but relaxed, particularly popular for lunches.
✉ 194 Jervois Road, Herne Bay,
☎ (09) 378 7811.

Mai Thai
Extremely friendly service and quality Thai food at reasonable prices. Private rooms available.
✉ corner Victoria and Albert Streets, central city, ☎ (09) 366 6258;
✉ also at St Heliers,
☎ (09) 585 1190.

Bolliwood
Distinctive décor and an extensive menu make this one of the city's leading Indian restaurants.
✉ 110 Ponsonby Road,
☎ (09) 376 6477.

Lord Nelson
Another of the city's long-established and consistently reliable restaurants, noted in particular for its steaks.
✉ 37 Victoria Street,
☎ (09) 379 4564.

Kermadec
Long established, with distinctively Pacific décor, overlooking the Viaduct Harbour.
✉ 1st Floor, Viaduct Quay, corner Quay and Lower Hobson Streets,
☎ (09) 309 0412.

Veranda Bar & Grill
Dependable and reasonably priced, this is one of the city's best-known eateries.
✉ 279 Parnell Road,
☎ (09) 309 6289.

The Cube Bar & Café
Cheerful, Greek-run eatery with a very jolly atmosphere. Live music on Thursday nights.
✉ 103 Victoria Road, Devonport,
☎ (09) 445 4444.

The Esplanade Hotel
Fully refurbished Edwardian dining room, with polished floors and ornate furnishings. Dignified dining, right on the Devonport waterfront, opposite the ferry terminal.
✉ 1 Victoria Road, Devonport,
☎ (09) 445 1291.

McHughs of Cheltenham
Buffet lunches 7 days a week, in a lovely Victorian-era dining room, with stunning views over Cheltenham Beach and the Rangitoto Channel.
✉ 46 Cheltenham Road, Devonport,
☎ (09) 445 0305.

The Hunting Lodge
A popular country restaurant, well worth the 40-minute drive. Set amid the vineyards of the Matua Valley, the lodge serves lunches and dinners with fine wines in a sylvan setting.

EATING OUT

✉ Waikoukou Valley Road, Waimauku (off SH16),
☎ (09) 411 8259.

• **BUDGET**

All parts of Auckland abound in takeaway bars, serving varieties of fast food. Traditional Kiwi takeaways such as pies and fish and chips have been joined in recent years by ethnic takeaways such as Chinese, Indian and Thai, along with hamburgers, pizzas, shish kebabs and fried chicken. For those who are more discerning, even when having takeaways, here are some recommendations.

• **FISH AND CHIPS**

The following places are recommended:

Catch 22

Some of the most delectable snapper and chips you can find. Cross Victoria Road with your parcel and eat them on the sea wall at Devonport.
✉ 19 Victoria Road, Devonport,
☎ (09) 445 2225.

Auckland Fish Market

Cafés, sushi bars and restaurants within this market serve fresh fish prepared and served in a variety of ways, in a location where parking is plentiful.
✉ 22 Jellicoe Street, Freemans Bay,
☎ (09) 379 1490.

Ponsonby Fresh Fish and Chip Company

✉ 127 Ponsonby Road,
☎ (09) 378 7885.

Mission Bay Fisheries

✉ 19/17 Tamaki Drive, Mission Bay,
☎ (09) 528 3361.

• **PIES**

Along with most other foods, Auckland's pies have made giant strides over the last few years, since the days when they could most charitably be described as 'mystery packs'. Now there are some luscious gourmet pies to be had, and eaten in a prime location such as the waterfront. And even a gourmet pie costs only about $3.50.

Narrow Neck Beach Café

Here the pies are so popular that if you don't get in before 13:00, the pie warmer will be almost empty. There's a tempting selection of fillings, and eating them overlooking Narrow Neck Beach is a divine experience.
✉ Old Lake Road, Narrow Neck Beach, North Shore,
☎ (09) 445 1096.

Ponsonby Pies

Also recommended for their great pies.
✉ 288 Ponsonby Road,
☎ (09) 361 3685.

What to Drink

What to Drink

The establishment of a thriving New Zealand wine industry in the last 20 years has been a major success story for local horticulture. New Zealand wines are now exported to many countries around the world, with Chardonnays and Sauvignon Blancs to the fore. Although the main grape-growing regions today are Marlborough, in the northeast of the South Island, and Hawkes Bay and Gisborne in the North Island, the western districts of Auckland were the cradle of New Zealand viticulture and remain significant producers today.

The pioneers of local wine-making were immigrants from war-torn Dalmatia, on the Adriatic coast, who came to the Northland and Auckland regions in the last decades of the 19th century, where they made a meagre income digging for fossilized gum from ancient kauri trees. The kauri gum, found in swamps in the northern parts of New Zealand, was used mainly for making varnish. As the gum became scarce, the Dalmatian immigrants – known locally as 'Dallies' – turned their hands to grape-growing and wine-making, skills used for generations in their European homeland. They found that Auckland's temperate maritime climate was ideal for growing white grapes, particularly in the valleys of west Auckland, which were sheltered from the prevailing cool, moist southwesterly winds.

The immigrants bought parcels of marginal land, mainly in the west Auckland districts of Henderson and Kumeu, planted them in vines and from the grape varieties made sweetish wines and sherries. For

Above: *This wine shop's stock includes a wide range of local vintages.*

Beers and Breweries

Auckland's balmy climate lends itself readily to **beer** consumption. Two large breweries, Lion Breweries and DB Breweries, dominate local production, but there are a number of boutique breweries such as the Loaded Hog Group and the Hauraki Brewing Company whose ales and lagers are more distinctive and diverse. Of Auckland's boutique brews, none is more iconic than Bean Rock Lager, named after Bean Rock, a lighthouse-topped rock in the Waitemata Harbour. Steinlager and DB Export Dry are the best known of the New Zealand lagers, but overseas brand lagers such as Stella Artois and Heineken are brewed locally and are also very popular.

EATING OUT

Above: *Vineyards on Waiheke Island.*

many years these were the only local wines marketed. However, with the increasingly discerning palates of New Zealanders as world travel increased and tastes became more sophisticated, a demand for better quality wines arose, and was met by producers. Better varieties of vines were planted and more subtle wines made from them. Wine production remained largely in the hands of second- and third-generation Dalmatian families, such as the Nobilos, Mazurans, Brajkoviches, Babiches and Soljans. The vineyards and wineries of west Auckland, for a long time a distinctive part of the landscape, were expanded and modernized. By the 1980s New Zealand wines were being marketed internationally and praised for their freshness and originality.

Today, in spite of Auckland's urban sprawl, which has overtaken much of the land formerly planted in vines, there are still vineyards and wineries in west Auckland. The larger wineries now depend on much of their supply from regions such as Gisborne and Hawkes Bay, however. In other developments, Auckland's traditional grape-growing districts have been joined by newer areas such as Matakana, near Warkworth, north of Auckland, in the Clevedon Valley, south of the city, and on Waiheke Island in the Hauraki Gulf (see Waiheke, page 80). Many of these wineries can be visited, the wines tasted and bought at discounted prices. Many wineries also arrange for their wine to be shipped overseas to the visitors' homes. Auckland's best-known labels are Corbans, Nobilo, Coopers Creek and Matua Valley, and from Waiheke Island, Stonyridge and Goldwater Estate.

Galbraith Brewing Company

Opened in the mid-1990s and built inside a former public library, Galbraith's is one of the city's most notable public houses. Here English-style 'real ales' are brewed and served in a spacious, wood-panelled environment. All the ales are top-fermented, unfiltered and unpasteurized and, also in English pub style, are served without carbonation, straight from the cask. The range of traditional ales at Galbraith's is complemented by an extensive lunch and dinner menu.
✉ 2 Mount Eden Road, Mount Eden
☎ (09) 379 3557
📠 (09) 307 6721
🖥 www.alehouse.co.nz
✉ real.ale@xtra.co.nz

WINERIES

WINERIES

For guided tours of Auckland's wineries:
☎ / 📠 (09) 849 4519
Freephone 0800 021 111, 🖥 www.insidertouring.co.nz

Manukau City
Villa Maria Winery

Five minutes drive from Auckland Airport. Tastings and guided winery tours.
✉ 118 Montgomery Drive, Mangere,
☎ (09) 255 0660
🕘 09:00–18:00 weekdays, 10:00–18:00 weekends.

Henderson District
Babich Wines Ltd

Tasting, cellar sales, picnics and mail orders.
✉ Babich Road, Henderson,
☎ (09) 833 7859,
🕘 09:00–17:00 Mon–Fri, 09:00–18:00 Sat, 11:00–17:00 Sun,
🖥 www.babichwines.co.nz

Lincoln Vineyards

Tastings, cellar sales.
✉ 130 Lincoln Road, Henderson,
☎ (09) 838 6944,
🕘 09:00–17:00 Mon–Fri, 10:00–17:00 Sat and 12:00–16:00 Sun.

Kumeu–Huapai District
Coopers Creek

Tastings, cellar sales, picnic area with barbecue facilities.
✉ SH16, Huapai North, ☎ (09) 412 8560, 🕘 09:30–17:30 Mon–Fri, 10:30–17:30 Sat and Sun.

Matua Valley Wines

Tastings, cellar sales and mail order sales.
✉ Waikoukou Valley Road, Waimauku, off SH16, ☎ (09) 411 8301, 🕘 10:00–17:00 Mon–Sun. 🍽 restaurant and picnic area.

Nobilo Group

Tastings, cellar sales, mail orders.
✉ 45 Station Road, Huapai, off SH16,
☎ (09) 412 6666,
🖥 www.nobilo.co.nz
🕘 09:00–17:00 Mon–Fri, 10:00–17:00 Sat and Sun.

Wine Trail Tours
Scenic wine-tasting tours. Sightseeing and wine-tasting combinations available.
☎ (09) 630 1540
📠 (09) 630 6157
🖥 www.winetrailtours.co.nz ✉ john@winetrailtours.co.nz

Fine Wine Tours
Tours of Auckland's leading wineries. Transport from the central city by coach.
☎ / 📠 (09) 849 4519
🖥 www.insidertouring.co.nz ✉ phil.parker@xtra.co.nz

Clevedon Valley
(Map D–D5)
The newest wine-growing district in the Auckland area. The valley's sheltered, sunny slopes are well-suited to the growing of vines. The village also has cafés and shops.

Arahura Vineyard: A boutique winery offering tastings and sales.
✉ Ness Valley Road, Clevedon ☎ (09) 292 9223 ✉ wines@arahuravineyard.co.nz
🕘 09:00–18:00 Sat–Sun, or by appointment

Inverness Estate: Attractive and historic grounds with accommodation. Visits by appointment only.
✉ Ness Valley Road
☎ (09) 292 8710

Eating Out

Shakespeare Tavern & Brewery

The Shakespeare brewery is located inside the Shakespeare Tavern, which is also one of Auckland's oldest licensed premises. Having survived the destruction of so many Victorian inner-city pubs during the 70s and 80s, the Shakespeare became the site of New Zealand's first mini-brewery. Brewing takes place in the bar, right under the eyes of the patrons, producing a stream of unfiltered and non-pasteurized beers by a traditional batch-brewing process. Seasonal and novelty beers such as Puck's Fundamental and Falstaff's Real Ale are also available.
✉ 61 Albert Street
☎ (09) 373 5396
📠 (09) 373 5397

Where to Drink

Until about 20 years ago, drinking in New Zealand was done in large, cheerless bars, known as 'booze barns'. Beer was poured from plastic hoses and food was restricted to pies, sausage rolls and chips. The behaviour tended to match the conditions. Some years after the rest of the world realized that civilized surroundings encouraged civilized conduct, New Zealand began to catch up. Today, thankfully, the booze barns belong well and truly to the past. In Auckland they have been replaced with scores of intimate, comfortable bars, many of which serve snacks and meals, and where music is as integral a part of the environment as the beers and wines that are served. There are now many 'boutique breweries' throughout New Zealand, and their products are on sale in most bars, on tap and in bottles. They make very refreshing drinking, many of them being organically brewed.

Most of the city's bars are in the central city, around the Viaduct Harbour and in Ponsonby, Parnell, Devonport and Takapuna. Most are open from early evening until late. A selection follows.

Right: *The Loaded Hog, right beside the Viaduct Harbour, is one of the city's busiest bars.*

WHERE TO DRINK

Deschlers
This bar has a jazz theme, a long servery, comfortable booths and a window seat which is the best spot in the city for people-watching. It is popular with all age groups. Live music is played on Mondays, Wednesdays and Saturdays.
✉ *17 High Street,*
☎ *(09) 379 6811.*

The Globe Bar
Has theme nights, a dance floor, pool tables as well as a big screen for viewing sports events.
✉ *Darby Street, central city,*
☎ *(09) 357 3980,*
🕒 *open from 16:00 until late.*

Bellini, Hilton Hotel
A special bar for a special occasion. Costly, but with incomparable views of the Waitemata Harbour right alongside.
✉ *Princes Wharf,*
☎ *(09) 978 2025.*

Iguacu Restaurant & Bar
Brasserie-style menu with inside and outside dining and great views of the city. Live jazz on Sundays.
✉ *269 Parnell Road, Parnell,*
☎ *(09) 358 4804.*

The Loaded Hog
A popular bar and restaurant right next to the Viaduct Harbour. Features naturally brewed beers and a cheerful menu.
✉ *204 Quay Street, waterfront,*
☎ *(09) 366 6491.*

The Immigrant Irish Bar
Cheap food (breakfast, lunch and dinner), Irish beer and live music Thursday–Sunday.
✉ *104 Fanshawe Street, city,*
☎ *(09) 373 2169.*

Claddagh Pub
Cosy and cheerfully atmospheric Irish bar.
✉ *372 Broadway, Newmarket,*
☎ *(09) 522 4410.*

The Dog's Bollix Bar & Band
The expansive interior of this Irish pub belies its exterior.
✉ *582 Karangahape Road, city,*
☎ *(09) 376 4600.*

Minus 5°
Everything in this bar is carved from hand-sculpted ice.
✉ *Princes Wharf, Quay Street,*
☎ *(09) 377 6702.*

Classic Comedy & Bar
This bar is a testing ground for established and aspiring comedians from Wednesdays to Saturdays.
✉ *321 Queen Street,*
☎ *(09) 373 4321.*

The Horse & Trap
An upmarket pub specializing in Monteiths premium beers and with a comprehensive menu.
✉ *3 Enfield Street, Mount Eden,*
☎ *(09) 630 3055.*

ENTERTAINMENT

Right: *The Sky City casino complex is open 24 hours a day, seven days a week.*

ENTERTAINMENT
Nightlife

Auckland's red-light districts are located in two areas of the city: the western end of Karangahape Road and in Fort Street, off Customs Street. In both districts there are all-night massage parlours and dance clubs, ranging from the sleazy to the stylishly raunchy. But visitors should be cautious if dropping into these areas very late at night, as both have more than their fair share of undesirable characters in the shadows.

For those who prefer clubs where watching is the main activity and the dancing is unencumbered by clothing, two city establishments stand out (*see side panel*).

Most of Auckland's **clubs** are located in the central city, at the high end of **Queen Street** and in the bohemian-like **Karangahape Road** (if you take a taxi, make sure that you tell the driver 'K-Road' as that's the name it's known by), which runs across the top of Queen Street. The clubs feature DJs mostly (bars and pubs are where the live bands play). The standard is impressive, with most local DJs being right up with the latest play from overseas. Clubbing starts late in Auckland (i.e. close to midnight) and most places are licensed until 06:00. A selection follows.

Showgirls

This well-run club features non-stop dancing. The décor is spangled and flashy, with generous use of mirrors, and if tipped the girls are not at all bashful.
✉ 55 Customs Street, city centre
☎ (09) 358 0245
🕐 11:00 until late
💲 $15 cover charge after 17:30
💻 www.showgirls.co.nz

The White House

Aficionados of unclothed entertainment rate this establishment highly. Located in what was once the Theosophical Society building, in keeping with its Washington DC theme, the White House includes a massage room called Monica's.
✉ 371 Queen Street
☎ (09) 377 4545
💻 www.thewhitehouse.co.nz

NIGHTLIFE

Karangahape Road

Calibre
Big booths and a cheerful ambience make this a drinking rather than a dance club these days.
✉ basement, 179 K-Road,
☎ (09) 303 1673,
🕐 00:00–08:00, Fri and Sat.

Kiss Bar
Non-stop pumping action in attractive and pleasant surroundings.
✉ 309 K-Road,
☎ (09) 303 2726,
💻 www.kissnightclub.co.nz

Ink
Comes with a dance floor, a snug bar and a courtyard at the back for fresh air.
✉ 268 K-Road,
☎ (09) 358 5103,
🕐 21:00–03:00 Thu, 21:00–06:00 Fri and Sat.

Club Raro
Popular with the Auckland Cook Islands community. Polynesian music and dancing.
✉ 318 Great South Road, Papatoetoe,
☎ (09) 278 7693,

Queen Street

Fu & Fu Bar
Underground in both senses. Noted for its music rather than its basic décor, DJs at Fu specialize in drum and bass and hip-hop.
✉ downstairs, 166 Queen Street,
☎ (09) 309 3079,
🕐 22:00–06:00 Tue–Sat (Fu Bar), 22:00 till late Fri and Sat (Fu).

Viaduct Harbour

Spy
Draws a rather different crowd to the K-Road scene, with members only at the weekends, but an amiable atmosphere with relaxed drinking.
✉ 204 Quay Street,
☎ (09) 377 7811,
🕐 21:00–03:00 Wed, 21:00–05:00 Thu, 21:00–06:00 Fri and Sat.

Sky City Casino

At the base of the Sky Tower, on the corner of Federal and Victoria Streets, is the Sky City Casino. A complex of two casinos, ten restaurants and bars, plus a hotel and theatre, the area is open 24 hours a day, seven days a week, catering to those who enjoy every type of gambling, from poker machines to roulette to blackjack. The main gaming floor is reached by an escalator from the ground floor of the Sky City building. The Alto Casino and Bar offers gambling in more intimate surroundings, with acts by local entertainers. A smart casual dress code applies in this part of the casino, though (no jeans).
Many of Auckland's bars contain an area where there are poker machines for the use of patrons.

ENTERTAINMENT

Aotea Centre
✉ the Edge in Aotea Square, 50 Mayoral Drive, just off Queen Street
☎ (09) 309 2677

Herald Theatre
✉ Aotea Centre, 50 Mayoral Drive
☎ (09) 309 2677

Sky City Theatre
✉ corner Victoria and Federal Streets
☎ (09) 363 6000

Town Hall
✉ 303 Queen Street
☎ (09) 309 2677

Silo Theatre
✉ Lower Greys Avenue
☎ (09) 366 0339

Civic
✉ corner of Queen and Wellesley Streets
☎ (09) 309 2677

Maidment Arts Centre
✉ 8 Alfred Street, University of Auckland campus
☎ (09) 308 2383

Lopdell House
✉ 418 Titirangi Road
☎ (09) 817 8087

Pump House
✉ Manurere Ave, Takapuna
☎ (09) 486 2386

Bruce Mason Centre
✉ corner Hurstmere Road and The Promenade, Takapuna
☎ (09) 488 2940

Theatres

The main venues for the performing arts are the **Aotea Centre**, the **Herald Theatre**, the **Sky City Theatre** and the beautifully refurbished **Town Hall** and the singular **Civic Theatre**. In these centres are held opera, classical music and chamber music performances, by both overseas and local groups. Outdoor rock and pop concerts are held mainly at **Ericsson Stadium**, and at **Western Springs Stadium** (which also doubles as a stockcar racing venue); indoor concerts are held at the **Civic**, a beautifully restored Art-Nouveau theatre complex. The Civic is also one of the venues for the **Auckland Film Festival**, held every July, and this theatre's Winter Garden – flamboyant galleries, Arabian Nights embellishments and recreated heavens and galaxies – make it a unique experience in the world of cinema.

Live theatre, for some years the one branch of the performing arts in which Auckland fell behind the rest of New Zealand, now thrives again thanks mainly to the work of the Auckland Theatre Company, whose plays are performed in the **Maidment Theatre**, and at the more intimate

Theatres and Cinemas

Left: *One of Auckland's several cinema complexes.*
Opposite: *The lovingly restored Civic, the city's oldest theatre.*

Herald and **Silo Theatres**. **Lopdell House** and the **Pump House** are two smaller suburban art and drama centres, while the **Bruce Mason Centre** is the North Shore's largest performing arts and convention venue.

Cinemas

There are several cinema complexes throughout Auckland, along with some surviving single-movie houses. The best of the latter are **The Bridgeway**, **Academy Cinema** and **Lido Cinema**. **Hollywood Cinema** screens classic movies at the weekends.

Of the larger companies, the **Berkeley group** has movie houses at Botany Downs, Mission Bay, Takapuna and Whangaparaoa, and **Sky City** has cinemas on Broadway, Newmarket, at Manukau City, Highland Park, Queen Street, Westgate and West City. **Rialto Cinemas** and **Hoyts Cinemas** are also popular.

The Entertainment pages of the *New Zealand Herald* carry daily listings of what's on at all of Auckland's theatres and cinemas, while the monthly magazine *Citymix*, available at newsstands, gives details of films, plays, exhibitions and concerts. A useful website is www.flicks.co.nz.

The Bridgeway
✉ 122 Queen Street, Northcote, North Shore
☎ (09) 418 3308

Academy Cinema
✉ Auckland Public Library Building, 64 Lorne Street, central city
☎ (09) 373 2761

Lido Cinema
✉ 427 Manukau Road, Epsom
☎ (09) 630 1500

Hollywood Cinema
✉ 20 St Georges Road, Avondale
☎ (09) 828 8393

Berkeley Cinemas
🖥 www.berkeleycinemas.co.nz

Sky City Cinemas
🖥 www.skycitycinemas.co.za

Rialto Cinemas
✉ 167–169 Broadway, Newmarket
☎ (09) 529 2218

Hoyts Cinemas
✉ Wairau Park, North Shore
☎ (09) 003 3309

ENTERTAINMENT

Auckland's Events Calendar

The following events are the most popular (exact dates vary slightly from year to year):

January
Horse-racing, Ellerslie.
Great Fitzroy Mussel Fest, Great Barrier Island.
ASB Classic Tennis, premier women's competition, ASB Tennis Centre, the Strand, Parnell.
Starbucks Music in Parks, various venues.
Heineken Open Men's Tennis, ASB Tennis Centre, the Strand, Parnell.
International cricket, Eden Park.
Big Day Out – Rock Music Festival, Ericsson Stadium, Penrose.
New Zealand Herald Auckland Anniversary Regatta.

February
Sky City Starlight Symphony, Auckland Domain.
Waiheke Island Food and Wine Festival.
Montana Mission Bay Jazz and Blues Streetfest, Mission Bay waterfront.
Devonport Food and Wine Festival.
Asian Lantern Festival, Albert Park.
Bike the Bays, Tamaki Drive, eastern water front.
Teddy Bears Picnic, Auckland Domain.
Opening matches of Super 14 rugby tournament, featuring the Auckland Blues.

March
Horse Racing, Onetangi beach, Waiheke Island.
Auckland Festival (of the Arts, Potters Park, Mount Eden.
Pasifika – celebration of Polynesian music, arts and culture, Western Springs Park.
St Patrick's Day Festival, Queen Street.
Nestlé Round the Bays Run.
ASB Secondary Schools Maori & Pacific Islands Performing Arts Festival, Manukau Sports Bowl, Manukau City.
Waiheke Jazz Festival.

April
Propecia Rally of New Zealand, outlying rural districts.
TV2 International Laugh Festival, various venues.

May
Auckland Writers' and Readers' Festival.
Finals of Super 14 Rugby.
New Zealand Boat Show, Auckland Showgrounds.

July
The Auckland Film Festival, Civic Theatre and other venues.

August
National Provincial Rugby Championship begins, Eden Park and North Harbour Stadium.

September
Going West Literary Festival, Titirangi War Memorial Hall, South Titirangi Road.

October
National Provincial Rugby Championship finals.
L'Oreal New Zealand Fashion Week, the Edge, Town Hall, Aotea Square.
Lindauer Coastal Classic, annual Auckland to Russell (Bay of Islands) yacht race.

November
BMW Auckland Marathon, Auckland waterfront.
Boost Mobil V8 Supercars, Pukekohe Raceway.
Auckland Philharmonia Spring Season, Auckland Town Hall.
Parnell Festival of Roses, Dove Meyer Rose Garden, Parnell.
Ellerslie Flower Show, Botanical Gardens, Manukau.
Grey Lynn Festival
Farmers Santa Parade, Queen Street.

December
Karekare Beach horse races.
A Cathedral Christmas, Holy Trinity Cathedral, Parnell.
Starbucks Music in Parks, various venues.
Auckland International Airport Three Day Equestrian Meeting, Puhinui Reserve.
Auckland Cup Carnival, Alexandra Park.
Coca Cola Christmas in the Park, Auckland Domain.
Horse-racing: the Auckland Cup, Ellerslie, (Boxing Day).
Summer Festival, Viaduct Harbour.

AUCKLAND'S EVENTS CALENDAR

Auckland's Events Calendar

Auckland's events calendar gets more crowded every year. Festivals, concerts, operas, yacht races, fashion shows, rugby, dance, running, recitals, horse racing, car rallying, tennis tournaments, cricket tests: almost every week of every month there's something to watch or participate in. For detailed information: Jasons Guides publishes a monthly guide called *Auckland – What's On* (www.jasons.com), *Auckland A–Z* contains lists of upcoming events, along with maps of the Auckland region (www.aucklandtourism.co.nz) and *Citymix* magazine, a monthly publication, provides detailed background stories on Auckland events, along with listings of these happenings (www.citymixmagazine.co.nz). These publications are also all available from the city's Information Centres. For further information on what to do in the city, visit www.hotcity.co.nz and www.eventsauckland.com

Festivals

Summertime is festival time in Auckland. From January through to Easter there are a number of festivals which celebrate Auckland's wine, food, music and cultures.

The Auckland Regatta
Friday 18 September, 1840.
'As it was wished to make this somewhat of a holiday, the gentlemen got up a boat race among themselves.' (from the Journal of Sarah Mathew, wife of the Surveyor-General of Auckland).
This first recorded boat race on Auckland's Waitemata Harbour occurred on the afternoon of the city's inception. Rowing boats, whaleboats and Maori canoes raced on the water that afternoon, following a ceremony in which the Union Jack was raised and toasts made to the young Queen Victoria. There has been an annual boat race on the Waitemata Harbour every year since. The Auckland Anniversary Regatta, held on the last Monday in January, is said to be the largest one-day boat race in the world.

Left: *Young cross-country runners compete in a city park.*

ENTERTAINMENT

Starlight Symphony concerts
✉ Auckland's Domain
🕓 Late afternoon, early evening, one night in December and again in late January or early February.

Montana Mission Bay Jazz and Blues Streetfest
✉ Mission Bay, Tamaki Drive
🕓 Early February, from 19:00 until midnight
💻 www.jazzandbluesstreetfest.com

Devonport Wine and Food Festival
✉ Windsor Reserve, Devonport
🕓 Early February, 10:30–18:30 (Sat), 10:30–17:00 (Sun)
💻 www.devonportwinefestival.co.nz

Starlight Symphony concerts

Auckland's Domain becomes a huge auditorium when the Auckland Philharmonia and various performers hold a free concert under the stars. Over 200,000 people gather on the grassy expanse in the Domain to have a picnic and watch the on-stage performances, which include Christmas carols in December, and classical, choir, country and western and rock numbers in January–February. The concerts are capped off with spectacular laser light and firework displays which erupt across the night sky.

The Montana Mission Bay Jazz and Blues Streetfest

This celebration takes place along the waterfront at Mission Bay. Tamaki Drive becomes a traffic-free zone during the evening, while jazz and blues groups perform along the waterfront drive. It is the perfect venue for a musical evening, with moonlight rippling across the water and the street's cafés and restaurants bustling with winers and diners.

Devonport Wine and Food Festival

A score of food stalls, a selection of wines, and diverse musical entertainment on two stages make this one of Auckland's liveliest and most popular gourmet festivals.

Lantern Festival

Held to celebrate the Chinese New Year, this is the main cultural celebration of Auckland's large Chinese population. Paper lanterns and dragons glow, woks sizzle and Chinese song, dance, fortune-telling and martial arts take place under the night sky.

FESTIVALS

Pasifika Festival
This cultural celebration attracts thousands of visitors and is one of the most colourful events on Auckland's calendar. Several stages are set up around the lake in Western Springs Park where stirring performances of Maori, Samoan, Tongan, Cook Island, Niuean and Tokelau Island songs, dances and drumming take place during the day. Traditional Pacific food, arts and crafts and music are sold at dozens of stalls spread around the park.

Above: *Young Samoan Aucklanders at the annual secondary schools' cultural festival.*

Auckland Secondary Schools Maori and Pacific Island Festival
Over 162 cultural groups and 13,000 students from 52 schools across Auckland perform on five separate stages – Maori, Cook Islands, Niuean, Samoan and Tongan – over three days. The festival keeps alive the different South Pacific cultures for its mainly Auckland-born, teenage participants.

Waiheke Jazz Festival, Waiheke Island
Jazz buffs can indulge their musical tastes for three and a half days over the Easter holiday weekend on Waiheke Island. The venues are characteristically unconventional: the local and overseas musicians strut their stuff in a tent, a café and a school hall, performing everything from Dixie to Blues to contemporary jazz. With Waiheke's established reputation as a wine-producing island, there are plenty of great local vintages to drink in too, along with the music. The island now also hosts a wine festival in early February.

Lantern Festival
✉ Albert Park
🕒 17:00–22:30 Fri, Sat and Sun evening, mid-February
💻 www.aucklandcity.govt.nz/whatson/events/lantern/default.asp

The Pasifika Festival
✉ Western Springs Park
🕒 A weekend in early March.

Auckland Secondary Schools Maori and Pacific Island Festival
✉ Manukau Sports Bowl, Manukau City
🕒 March

Waiheke Jazz Festival
✉ Waiheke Island
🕒 Easter weekend
💻 www.waihekejazz.co.nz

EXCURSIONS

Wenderholm Regional Park

Wenderholm Regional Park
Location: Map D–B3
Distance from city: 30km (19 miles)
☎ (09) 426 1200
🕒 06:00–21:00 (summer), 06:00–19:00 (winter)
🍽 Barbecue facilities.

Couldrey House
✉ Wenderholm Regional Park
☎ (09) 303 1530
🕒 13:00–16:00 weekends only
💰 adults $2, children 50c

Waiwera Infinity Thermal Resort & Spa
✉ 7–11 Waiwera
☎ (09) 426 5369
📞 (09) 426 4730
✉ jdb@waiwera.co.nz
🕒 09:00–22:00, daily

Below: *The Victorian era Couldrey homestead, in Wenderholm Regional Park, north of Auckland.*

About 45 minutes' drive north of the city, over the hill from the estuary of the Waiwera River, is Wenderholm Regional Park. Leave the Northern Motorway, drive through Orewa, and then continue north on SH1 for about eight minutes. Reached by a long straight driveway, Wenderholm consists of a sheltered estuary lying alongside an expanse of grass covered by pohutukawa trees, where there are picnic and barbecue facilities, fronted by a wide, safe swimming beach. There is also a testing, but well-worth-the-effort, signposted walk to the top of the headland at the southern end of the park, from where there are sublime views of Whangaparaoa Bay and Motuora and Kawau Islands. Sited attractively near the base of the hill at Wenderholm's southern end is **Couldrey House**, a preserved Victorian farmhouse whose rooms and displays show how Auckland's pioneer families lived. If it's a cool day, a visit to the **Waiwera Thermal Resort and Spa**, just over the hill from the park, is a warmly relaxing experience.

WENDERHOLM & MATAKANA

Matakana to Tawharanui

An hour's drive north from Auckland, the Matakana area is reached via the riverside town of **Warkworth**. At the roundabout at the northern end of the town, turn right onto Matakana Road. Five minutes' drive further on is the picturesque **Matakana district**, where there are several vineyards and, at the weekends in the village, a craft market and a farmers market specializing in organic foods.

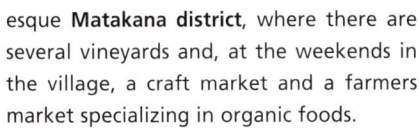

The six vineyards on the Matakana Wine Trail are: **Ransom Wines**, just south of Warkworth town, then in Matakana itself, **Acension Vineyard and Café**, **Matakana Estate**, **Hyperion Wines**, **Heron's Flight Vineyard and Café** and **Mahurangi Estate**.

A short drive further on is **Tawharanui Regional Park**, one of the loveliest stretches of coastline in the region. Turn right at Omaha Flats, drive through Takatu and follow the road to the end of the peninsula, to Tawharanui. Here there is excellent swimming and picnicking.

Back on the Matakana Road, another recommended excursion is to continue driving north for a short time, calling in at pretty **Mathesons Bay**, the fishing village of **Leigh** and over a hill to **Goat Island Marine Reserve**, where it's possible to swim among the fish. A short drive further on is the long, sweeping surf beach **Pakiri**.

Above: *Tawharanui Regional Park, east of Warkworth, is about a 1¼ hour drive north from Auckland.*

Matakana
Location: Map D–B2
Distance from city: 45km (28 miles)
✉ Matakana Road (east from Warkworth)
🖥 www.warkworth-information.co.nz
🖥 www.matakanawine.com

Tawharanui Regional Park
Location: Map D–C2
Distance from city: about 55km (34 miles)
✉ Takatu Road
☎ Parksline: (09) 303 1530
🖥 www.arc.govt.nz

EXCURSIONS

The Vineyards of Waiheke
Waiheke Island's climate is hotter and drier than that of Auckland city, and its warm maritime climate, sunny hill slopes and unique soils combine to produce ideal growing conditions for rich, lush, full-bodied wines, notably Cabernet blends, Syrah and Chardonnay. There are now 27 vineyards on the island, many of which are open to the public, and wine tastings and tours of the island can be taken. Some of the wineries have quality cafés attached to them. Waiheke's best-known labels are Goldwater Estate and Stonyridge. Te Whau Vineyard Café and the Mudbrick Vineyard and Restaurant are among the several vineyards also providing dining facilities. Every February Waiheke hosts a food and wine festival.
💻 www.waihekewine.co.nz

Waiheke Island
Location: Map D–D4

Waiheke Island Visitor Information Office:
✉ 2 Korora Road, Oneroa
☎ (09) 372 1234
💻 www.ki-wi.co.nz/waiheke.htm
💻 www.tourismwaiheke.co.nz

Waiheke

Waiheke is a large island – 92km^2 (36 sq miles) of rolling hills, stands of native bush, small settlements, vineyards and olive groves – a 35-minute fast ferry ride from Auckland. Its scalloped coastline has some superb sandy beaches, notably **Oneroa**, **Onetangi** and **Mawhitipana Bay** (Palm Beach).

Once a retreat for 'alternative lifestylers', Waiheke is now a dormitory suburb of Auckland city. Most people live at the western end of the island, where the main town of Oneroa and the ferry terminal at Matiatia are located. During summer, Waiheke's population swells substantially as vacationers occupy the island's many holiday houses. The variety of accommodation includes lodges, apartments and motels. The central parts of the island are undulating hill country and farmland, while at the elevated northwestern end is **Stony Batter**, a hill strewn with boulders from ancient volcanic explosions, and a World War II gun emplacement from where there are magnificent views of the Pacific Ocean.

Waiheke has many opportunities for outdoor activities, including sailing, sea kayaking, horse trekking and mountain biking. There are also some excellent walking tracks on the island.

WAIHEKE & TIRITIRI MATANGI

Tiritiri Matangi

Tiritiri Matangi, which means 'a place tossed or moved by the wind', is a small island with an indented coastline, off the tip of the **Whangaparaoa Peninsula**, 35km (22 miles) north of Auckland city. It is now a wildlife sanctuary where some of New Zealand's rarest birds can be readily observed in the wild from bush walkways. A volunteer native forest replanting scheme has, over the last few years, planted more than three million native trees, establishing a natural habitat for some of New Zealand's rarest native birds: bellbirds, little spotted kiwis, saddlebacks and stitchbirds, while the endangered takahe can also be observed on open ground.

From the **Hauraki Gulf** the steep-sided island of **Little Barrier** can be clearly seen on a fine day. Called Hauturu by Maori, Little Barrier contains the largest remaining area of relatively unmodified northern New Zealand forest. Since 1885 it has been a sanctuary for critically endangered bird species such as kakapo, kokako and stitchbirds, as well as New Zealand's unique fossil reptile, the tuatara. Access to Little Barrier is restricted to permit holders only.

The Takahe
Long thought to be extinct, the flightless native bird the takahe was rediscovered living in a remote valley of Fiordland, in the southwest of the South Island, in 1948. Also called the notornis, takahe are strictly protected today and live mainly in wildlife sanctuaries like Tiritiri Matangi island in the Hauraki Gulf, where they are able to roam freely. Standing out among the island's vegetation with their dark blue and turquoise plumage and bright red-orange beaks and legs, takahe are now breeding successfully on Tiritiri Matangi.

Tiritiri Matangi
Location: Map D–C3
Distance from city: 35km (22 miles)

Ferry Services
✉ To the island from Gulf Harbour Marina, on the Whangaparaoa Peninsula, or from Auckland city.
☎ (09) 367 9111

Opposite: *A typically secluded bay on Waiheke Island.*
Left: *A tuatara on Little Barrier Island, a wildlife sanctuary near Auckland.*

EXCURSIONS

Great Barrier
Location: Map D–E1
Distance from city: about 90km (60 miles)

Hauraki Gulf Visitor Informatiion Centre
✉ Claris, Great Barrier Island
☎ (09) 429 0033
📠 (09) 429 0660
💻 www.aucklandnz.com

Great Barrier

Largest and most distant of the Hauraki Gulf islands, Great Barrier is about 90km (60 miles) northeast of Auckland and connected to the city by fast, modern ferries. The island's relative remoteness, serenity and easy-going way of life make it a haven for those wanting to get away from the pressures of urban living.

Of volcanic origin and once the site of a whaling station, Great Barrier has a mountainous interior still clothed in native forest, a deeply indented coastline on its western side and spectacularly beautiful white sand beaches on its eastern coast. Swimming, surfing and diving are ideal along this coast, especially at **Medlands Beach**.

Kauri forests once covered the island's interior. On the flanks of Great Barrier's central peak, **Mount Hobson**, are the remains of dams that were used to impound its streams, then 'tripped' to flush kauri logs down to the coast. The logs were rafted and floated to sawmills. The dams can be reached by steep walking tracks from the coast.

The largest settlement on Great Barrier is **Tryphena**, but there is also basic accommodation at **Whangaparapara** and **Port Fitzroy**. There are also air connections from Auckland to the island.

Right: *Medlands, one of Great Barrier Island's finest east coast beaches.*

GREAT BARRIER & KAWAU

Kawau

This densely wooded island is reached by ferry from Auckland city or the Sandspit, near Warkworth. A very hilly island, Kawau is deeply penetrated on its western side by sheltered **Bon Accord Harbour**. Steep, bush-covered hills plunge to a mainly rocky coast, although there are exposed beaches on the island's eastern coast and at the northwestern extremity. Excellent walking tracks, mainly through kanuka bush and some regenerating native forest, crisscross the island, but there are no public roads. Most residents rely on launches and ferries for transport.

Kawau has a fascinating history. In the 19th century, copper was mined here and the remains of the copper smelter can still be seen. The island was also home to **Sir George Grey**, Governor of New Zealand from 1845–53 and 1861–68. He built a luxurious home at **Mansion House Bay**, on Kawau's southeastern coast, and introduced exotic animals, plants and trees to the island. Wallabies (now considered a pest), kookaburras and peacocks still live on the island, and Grey's handsome, restored **Mansion House** can be visited by the public.

Above: The restored Mansion House, home of one-time Governor of New Zealand, Sir George Grey. The house, beside a bay on Kawau Island, is open to the public.

Kawau
Location: Map D–C2
Distance from city: about 50km (30 miles) east of Warkworth, in Kawau Bay

Kawau Kat Cruises
✉ Sandspit Wharf and Pier 3 Ticket Office, Quay Street, Warkworth
☎ (09) 425 8006
📠 (09) 425 7650
💻 www.kawaukat.co.nz

Mansion House
✉ Mansion House Bay, Kawau Island
☎ (09) 422 8882
🕘 09:30–15:30, daily
💰 $4 adults, $2 children

TRAVEL TIPS

Above: Bus transport is the most common form of public transport in and around Auckland.

Etiquette
Auckland is a very informal city, and the only special protocol to be observed is if one is officially visiting a Maori marae, a centre of Maori tribal life. When visiting Auckland's many regional parks, ensure that you respect the anti-litter rules and fire regulations, the conservation regulations of the marine parks and comply with the fishing and shellfish gathering limits, which are clearly sign-posted throughout coastal areas.

Best Times to Visit

The second half of summer – February to April – sees Auckland at its best. The weather at this time is more settled and less humid than in December and January, the Christmas rush is over and the schools have reopened, bringing less pressure on recreational areas. During February and March the daytime temperatures are still consistently in the 20–24°C (68–75°F) range, meaning that the sea temperatures are also warm and the evenings settled and light enough for barbecues and other outdoor activities. February and March are also the festival months, bringing a great variety of outdoor concerts and cultural celebrations. April to June are the autumn months, when temperatures are cooler and the days shorter, but these are also pleasant months, drier and with daytime temperatures still mild. The only really cool and wet months are July, August and September.

i SITE Visitors Centres

These are located throughout the Auckland region and are denoted by a green, italicized *i*. The centres offer detailed and impartial information about all aspects of accommodation, car rentals, tours and transport. Contacts: ✉ SkyCity, Princes Wharf, Auckland International and Domestic Airports, ☎ (09) 979 2333, ℻ (09) 979 2334. North Shore Visitor Information Centre, ✉ 49 Hurstmere Road, Takapuna, ☎ (09) 486 8670. ✉ 3 Victoria Road, Devonport, ☎ (09) 446 0677. ✉ 2 Korora Road, Oneroa, Waiheke Island, ☎ (09) 372 1234, ℻ (09) 372 9919. ✉ Claris, Great Barrier

TRAVEL TIPS

Island, ☎ (09) 429 0033, ✆ (09) 429 0660. 🖥 www.aucklandnz.com 🖥 www.aucklandtourism.co.nz
Reservations: ✉ reservations@aucklandnz.com

Entry Requirements

Visitors to New Zealand must have a passport, valid for three months beyond the intended time of stay. If the visitor's home country has a consulate in Auckland, which can renew the passport, one month beyond the time of stay is sufficient. Consulate offices in Auckland are listed under 'Diplomatic and Consular Representatives' in the Yellow Pages of the Auckland telephone directory, and include the US and Canada, most European and several Asian countries. Visitors from the UK are automatically entitled to stay for up to six months in New Zealand, and a three-month permit is granted to citizens of most European and Southeast Asian countries, Japan, the US and Canada. Australian citizens and permanent residents can stay indefinitely. Citizens of other countries must obtain a visa, valid for three months, from a New Zealand embassy. For information on embassies contact the Ministry of Foreign Affairs and Trade, ✉ enquiries@mfat.govt.nz 🖥 www.mfat.govt.nz

Departure Tax

Departure tax from Auckland International Airport is $25 per passenger, payable at the airport.

Customs

There are excellent duty-free shops and generous duty-free allowances for travellers entering New Zealand at Auckland International Airport. For example there is a $700 passenger concession for duty-free purchases, and if this is not exceeded two 1125ml bottles of spirits can be imported, also free of duty. For Customs and Immigration, proceed down the escalator to the Customs-Immigration check-points. The baggage carousels are directly behind the check-points and spread across the Customs hall. Your flight details and the allocated carousel for your flight will be shown on the monitor screens behind the customs point. Collect your baggage and proceed out of the terminal either by the Green Lane (nothing to declare) or the Red Lane (something to declare). If you need assistance at the airport, ask a **Hospitality Ambassador** (who will be wearing a bright blue jacket) or a **Customer Services Officer** (wearing a red jacket) to help you.

Travel Tips

Health Requirements

No vaccinations are required prior to visiting New Zealand. However there are stringent regulations to protect against the importation of agricultural diseases such as foot and mouth, which would be catastrophic for the farming sector. Visitors are required to declare whether they are in possession of agricultural equipment or have visited an overseas farm recently, and the importation of fresh fruit, honey, vegetables or meat is prohibited. Goods made from endangered species, such as whale bone or teeth, cannot be brought into New Zealand under an international agreement. A Customs Declaration Form must be filled in on arrival and kept until the Customs hall has been passed through. There are severe penalties for any infringement of the Customs laws.

Getting There

The main point of entry to New Zealand is Auckland International Airport, at Mangere, to the southwest of the city. A modern, user-friendly facility, the airport contains a comprehensive range of services, with particularly good shopping precincts.

Airline and Airport Information, 24 hours, ☎ (09) 256 8899, ℘ (09) 275 5835, ✉ mail@akl-airport.co.nz 🖥 www.auckland-airport.co.nz

International Airlines:

Aerolines Argentinas, ☎ (09) 379 3675.
Aircalin, ☎ (09) 308 3363.
Air Canada, ☎ (09) 379 3371.
Air New Zealand International, ☎ (09) 357 3000.
Air Pacific, ☎ (09) 379 2404.
Air Vanuatu, ☎ (09) 373 3435.
American Airlines, ☎ (09) 309 9159.
British Airways, ☎ 0800 274 847.
Cathay Pacific Airways, ☎ (09) 379 0861.
China Airlines, ☎ (09) 308 3364.
Emirates ☎ (09) 968 2208.
Freedom Air, ☎ 0800 600 500.
Garuda Indonesia, ☎ (09) 366 1862.
Japan Airlines, ☎ (09) 379 9906.
Korean Air, ☎ (09) 307 3687.
Lufthansa Airlines, ☎ (09) 303 1529.
Malaysia Airlines, ☎ (09) 373 2741.
Pacific Blue Airlines ☎ 0800 67 00 00.
Polynesian Airlines, ☎ (09) 377 0644.
Qantas Airways, ☎ (09) 357 8900.
Royal Tongan Airlines, ☎ (09) 624 1160.
Singapore Airlines, ☎ (09) 303 2129.
Thai Airways, ☎ (09) 377 3886.
United Airlines, ☎ (09) 308 1747.

Domestic Airlines:

Air New Zealand National, Reservations and fare enquiries, ☎ 0800 737 000.
Flight Arrivals and

Travel Tips

Departures (24-hour), ☎ (09) 306 5560.
Qantas Airways, Reservations and fare enquiries, ☎ (09) 357 8900.
Flight Arrivals and Departures (24-hour), ☎ (09) 357 8900.
Auckland Airport Flight Information, ☎ (09) 256 8899.
Airport to City Connections: Both the international and domestic airports have taxi, shuttle bus and bus stops right outside their doors, and there is a free bus service from one terminal to the other, leaving every few minutes. The Air Bus links both airports to the city, leaving every 20 minutes, ☎ free 0508 247 287, 🖥 www.airbus.co.nz
Airport Super Shuttle: offers door-to-door, airport-hotel-airport transfers, ☎ (09) 306 3960, ✆ (09) 306 3959, Reservations: ✆ reservations@supershuttle.co.nz 🖥 www.supershuttle.co.nz
A taxi from the airport to the central city costs about $45. Departure tax is $25.
Cruises: The cruise ship season extends from December through to April, with most passenger ships tying up to Princes Wharf, right on the city's front doorstep.

What to Pack

Light clothes only are needed during the summer months, but the occasional wet period means that an umbrella also comes in very handy. Swimming gear, plus sunscreen, sun-hat and insect repellent are important accessories from December through April, and sturdy boots are recommended for hiking excursions. The winter months, from June through September, are cool, so if visiting at this time pack jackets, jumpers and a light topcoat. But as far as dress codes are concerned, Auckland

---

The Britomart Transport Centre

One of the bigger blunders in Auckland's 20th century development was the replacing of the city's main railway station, which for many years was located at the foot of Queen Street, with a station in Beach Road, in 1930. The new station was inconveniently located more than 1km (0.6 miles) away from the central business district. Ever since then, rail transport played a smaller and smaller part in the lives of Auckland commuters, who preferred first trams, then cars and buses, all of which could take them right into the heart of the city. However, with the completion in 2003 of the new integrated **Britomart Project**, built around the former Chief Post Office in Queen Elizabeth II Square at the foot of Queen Street, rail transport has once again become a public transport option for Aucklanders.

The Britomart project includes an underground rail station, a bus interchange, a Central Post Office building, an underground concourse connecting Queen Elizabeth II Square with the railway station and protection and restoration of the heritage buildings in the area.

Travel Tips

Banks
ANZ Banking Group (NZ) Ltd
☎ 0800 269 296
ASB Bank Ltd
☎ 0800 272 272
Bank of New Zealand
☎ 0800 800 468
Bankdirect
☎ 0800 500 400
HSBC
☎ (09) 915 4868
Kiwibank
☎ (09) 336 1133
National Bank of New Zealand
☎ 0800 18 18 18
TSB Bankdirect
☎ 0508 872 226
Westpac Trust
☎ 0800 400 600

Foreign Exchange
The following sell travellers cheques and foreign cash:
American Express
✉ 105 Queen Street, central city
☎ (09) 379 8286
✉ 67–69 Symonds Street
☎ (09) 367 4221
✉ Shop 126, Westfield Shoppingtown, St Lukes, Mount Albert
☎ (09) 815 6420
Thomas Cook Foreign Exchange
✉ 34 Queen Street
☎ (09) 377 2666
Travelex New Zealand Ltd
✉ 32 Queen Street
☎ (09) 358 9173
E-Trans International Finance Ltd
✉ 105 Queen Street
☎ (09) 379 8286

is the most informal of New Zealand cities, so the wearing of suits and ties is confined to the business sector.

Money Matters

The currency is the New Zealand dollar, divided into 100 cents. There are $100, $50, $20, $10 and $5 notes; gold coins in denominations of $2 and $1, silver 50 and 20 cents and an alloy 10 cent piece.

A practical aid for shoppers is the EFTPOS (Electronic Funds Transfer at Point of Sale) card system. Issued by the trading banks, an EFTPOS card deducts the relevant sum of money from a local cheque or savings account, after a PIN number is entered. Many EFTPOS holders will also issue cash on request. Nearly all Auckland shops, restaurants, hotels, motels and petrol stations have EFTPOS, enabling people to avoid carrying large amounts of cash and making the city an almost 'cashless' one.

A 12.5% **goods and services tax** known as GST is added to the cost of purchases and services, except goods in duty-free shops. The tax cannot be claimed back by overseas visitors, although some stores may export your purchases, so that they are exempt from GST.

Banks are open from 09:00–16:30 Monday–Friday. Most branches have Automatic Teller Machines on their outside wall to dispense cash 24 hours a day. They require a valid cash card (they accept most overseas credit cards) and PIN number.

Tipping is not a common custom in New Zealand and so is done entirely at the customer's discretion. A tip of 10% may be added to restaurant bills in return for particularly helpful service, for example.

Travel Tips

Transport

Motorists drive on the left-hand side of the road. Wearing of seat belts is compulsory at all times. No pedestrians or cyclists are allowed on motorways. Stopping of vehicles on motorways is prohibited at all times, except in emergencies. Reciprocal driving rights exist between New Zealand and most other countries. Most rental car companies will ask to see an International Driver's Licence. The driver must be over 21 years of age. For road rules and international driver licences, call the **Automobile Association**, ☎ (09) 377 4660.

Rental Cars: There are 27 pages of advertisements for rental car companies in the Yellow Pages. 🖥 www.yellowpages.co.nz Several rental car companies have offices at Auckland's International and Domestic Airports. Rental car rates start at $25 per day.

Bus and **train** services around the city have been greatly improved with the completion of the Britomart Centre (see panel, page 87), and there are excellent **ferry** services from central Auckland to various parts of the outer city: Stanley Bay, Bayswater, Devonport, Birkenhead, Half Moon Bay, Whangaparaoa and several of the islands of the Hauraki Gulf, with an especially frequent service to Waiheke Island. Auckland bus, ferry and train information, ☎ (09) 366 6400, 🖥 www.maxx.co.nz

Time Difference

Auckland and the rest of New Zealand is 12 hours ahead of GMT, and uses daylight saving time in the summer months. Clocks are put forward one hour in early October and back one hour in mid-March.

Communications

Public telephones take phone cards or credit cards, and local calls cost from 50 cents per call. Phone cards are available from convenience stores and service stations. ☎ 018 for directory assistance (within New Zealand), ☎ 0172 (international numbers). Long-distance calls (STD) and international calls (IDD) can be made from any public phone. Simply dial the area code, then the number, for calls within New Zealand. For international calls, dial 00, then the relevant country code, then the number. There are plenty of **post offices**, called New Zealand Post Shops, and posting boxes throughout Auckland. These offer stamp and stationery sales, parcel post, facsimile services, poste restante and

electronic express. Many post shops have Kiwibank services within their premises. It costs 45 cents to send a letter within New Zealand, ordinary post, 90 cents fast post (delivery next day within New Zealand). ⏲ 09:00–17:00, Monday–Friday, and some branches are open on Saturdays from 10:00–13:00.
Mail Service Centres: ✉ 167 Victoria Street, central city, ⏲ 07:30–19:30, Monday–Friday. Enquiries, NZ Post, ☎ 0800 501 501.
Mailing services delivery times: Australia and the South Pacific, 3–10 days; the rest of the world, 4–10 days.

Electricity

230 volts, 50 hertz, with three-pin power sockets.

Health Precautions

A very good public health system ensures that most visitors are treated quickly for serious sickness or injury, but a comprehensive travel insurance policy is essential to cover any illness, accident or theft of goods. Auckland's medical practitioners and medical centres are listed in the telephone book. Water is safe to drink from the tap everywhere. During the months from December through March, mosquitoes can be a nocturnal nuisance, and anti-mosquito remedies are available from hardware stores and pharmacies. It is also advisable to carry a general insect repellent when hiking in bush areas or staying near lakes or rivers. Strong, comfortable boots are recommended for bush walks.

The depletion of the ozone layer over Antarctica means that the Auckland sun can burn the human skin very quickly in summer, and a sunhat and broad-spectrum sun block are essential to protect against the ferocity of the sun's rays during outdoor activities.

Personal Safety

Auckland is plagued with the problems of large cities all over the world: traffic congestion, road rage, theft and violence. Most visitors will avoid these threats to their safety and security by exercising common-sense precautions.

Auckland city is not noted for the considerateness of its road signs, which are often hard to see or absent. It is therefore strongly advisable to obtain a good map of the central city and suburbs – one of the Wises' maps and guides is recommended – to help negotiate your way around what can be a confusing city, particularly in the suburbs. The standard of driving in Auckland is not impressive either, with lane changes and turns

Travel Tips

often not indicated. Try to avoid driving on the motorways at peak periods (07:30–09:00 and 16:30–18:30), when they often become gridlocked, and prepare to drive defensively at all times. Auckland can be a violent city after dark, especially when bars and pubs close, late at night. The most dangerous place in the city is the Downtown after midnight, where crimes of violence sometimes occur. Do not walk alone in the unlit parts of Auckland city late at night. Also, when visiting popular tourist spots such as the Waitakeres and west coast beaches by car, do not leave valuables in the vehicles, as these are an obvious target for thieves. Lock cars securely at all times.

Emergencies

Ambulance, Fire, Police: ☎ 111.
Accident and Emergency Clinics and Public Hospitals: Central City Auckland Hospital, ✉ Park Road, Grafton, ☎ (09) 379 7440.
Starship Children's Hospital, ✉ Park Road, Grafton, ☎ (09) 307 8900.
South Auckland Middlemore Hospital, ✉ Hospital Road, Otahuhu, ☎ (09) 276 0000.
North Shore Hospital, ✉ Shakespeare Road, Takapuna, ☎ (09) 486 8900.
Near the front of the Auckland Telephone Directory there is a full list of private accident and medical centres and doctors under the general heading, 'Registered Medical Practitioners & Medical Centres'.

Language

Both English and Maori are the official languages of New Zealand. English is universally spoken and understood.

Recommended Reading

History:
Palmer, David *Walking Historic Auckland* (New Holland).
Stewart, Graham *Auckland Before the Harbour Bridge* (Grantham House).
Stone, Russell *From Tamaki-Makau-Rau to Auckland* (Auckland University Press).
Wolfe, Richard *Auckland: A Pictorial History* (Random House).

Pictorial:
Baker, Ian *The Gulf: New Zealand's Hauraki Gulf Explored* (New Holland).
McCree, Bob *Auckland's Top Spots* (New Holland).
Shaw, Peter *Rainbow Over Mt Eden: Images of Auckland* (Godwit).

Literature:
Curnow, Allen *Allen Curnow – Selected Poems* (Penguin NZ).
Stead, CK *All Visitors Ashore* (Godwit).
Ireland, Kevin *Under the Bridge & Over the Moon* (Random House).

Recreational:
Dench, Alison and Parore, Lee-anne *Walking the Waitakere Ranges* (New Holland).
Vause, Helen *Walking Auckland* (New Holland).

Index of Sights

Name	Page	Map
Albert Park	21	A–D2
Aotea Centre	72	A–D3
Auckland Art Gallery Toi O Tamaki	39	A–D3
Auckland Cathedral of the Holy Trinity	39	A–F4
Auckland Domain	14	C–E6
Auckland Harbour Bridge	9	C–D5
Auckland Museum	14	A–E4
Auckland Regional Botanic Gardens	26	B–H6
Auckland Zoo	23	B–D1
Awhitu	25	D–B6
Browns Bay	35	C–D1
Campbells Bay	35	C–E2
Castor Bay	37	C–D3
Central City Library	28	A–D2
Cheltenham (Beach)	18	C–F5
City Art Gallery	21	A–D3
Civic Theatre	72	A–D3
Cornwall Park	29	B–E2
Cornwallis Park	33	B–A5
Cornwallis peninsula	33	B–A6
Devonport	18	C–E5
Dove Meyer Robinson Park	31	A–F2
Eden Garden	30	A–D6
Eden Park	43	B–D2
Ewelme Cottage	38	A–F4
Goat Island Marine Reserve	79	D–D3
Great Barrier (Island)	82	D–E1
Hauraki Gulf	36	D–D4
Hauraki Gulf Marine Park	37	D–D3
Highwic	38	A–E6
Howick Historical Village	39	B–I2
Hunua Ranges Regional Park	25	D–D6
Karangahape Road	51	A–C4
Karekare	19	D–A5
Kawau	83	D–C2
Kelly Tarlton's Antarctic Encounter and Underwater World	17	B–F1
Kinder House	31	A–F4

Name	Page	Map
Lake Pupuke	35	C–E3
Long Bay	26	C–D1
Mairangi Bay	35	C–D2
Mansion House	83	D–C3
Matakana	79	D–B2
Medlands Beach	82	D–F2
Milford	35	C–E3
Mission Bay	27	B–F1
Mount Eden	30	A–D6
Mount Hobson	82	A–F6
Mount Victoria	18	C–E5
Murrays Bay	35	C–D2
Museum of Transport and Technology (MOTAT)	22	B–D2
New Gallery	40	A–D3
New Zealand National Maritime Museum	20	A–D1
Northcote	38	C–D4
One Tree Hil	29	B–E3
Oneroa	80	D–D4
Onetangi	80	D–D4
Palm Beach	80	D–D4
Parnell Road	29	A–F3
Ponsonby	32	A–A2
Port Fitzroy	82	D–E1
Rangitoto Island	37	C–G4
Remuera	51	B–E2
Rothesay Bay	35	C–D2
Shakespear Regional Park	25	D–C4
Sky Tower	16	A–D2
Takapuna	34	C–E4
Tamaki Drive	27	C–G6
Tawharanui Regional Park	79	D–C2
Tiritiri Matangi	81	D–C3
Titirangi	33	B–B4
Torbay	35	C–D1
Town Hall	72	A–D3
Tryphena	82	D–F2
Viaduct Harbour	15	A–C1
Victoria Park Market	53	A–C2
Waiheke (Island)	80	D–D4
Waitakere Ranges	24	D–B5
Waitemata Waterfront	27	A–C1
Warkworth	79	D–C2
Wenderholm	78	D–B3
Westhaven Marina	41	C–D5

92

General Index

Page numbers given in **bold** type indicate photographs

A
Acacia Cottage 10, 29
accommodation **54**, 54–59
airports 86–87
Albany 34
Albert Park 7, 21, **21**
Alberton 38
Algie's Castle 47
America's Cup 15
amusement park 44
Anawhata 19
Antarctic 17
antiques 51
Aotea Centre 47, 72
Aotea Square 47
Aotea Square Market 53
Aotearoa 8
aquarium 17
aquatic centres 44
Arataki Environmental & Heritage Centre 24
art galleries *see* museums & galleries
arts 13, 39–40
Atkinson Park 35
Auckland Art Gallery Toi O Tamaki *see* museums & galleries
Auckland Cathedral of the Holy Trinity 39
Auckland City 11
Auckland Domain 7, 14
Auckland Film Festival 72
Auckland Harbour Bridge 9
Auckland Harbour Bridge Climb 44
Auckland Museum *see* museums & galleries
Auckland Regional Botanic Gardens 35
Auckland Secondary Schools Maori and Pacific Island Festival 77, **77**
Auckland Theatre Company 72
Auckland Zoo 23
Avondale Market 53
Awhitu (Regional Park) 25

B
banks 88
bars 66, 68, **68**, 69
Bastion Point 27, 48, **48**
Bay of Islands 9
beaches 19, **19**, 25, 26, **26**, 27, **27**, 33, 34, 42, 43, 80
beers 65
birds 81
Bishop Park Scenic Reserve 35
Black Rock 47
boat cruises *see* cruises
boating *see* sailing
Bon Accord Harbour 83
bookshops 52
botanic gardens 26
breweries 65, 66, 68
Britomart Transport Centre 87
Browns Bay 35
Bruce Mason Centre 36, 72, 73
Bucklands Beach 42
buildings 38–39
bungy jump 16
Bungy Sky Screamer 44

C
Calliope Wharf 18
Campbells Bay 35
campsites 25
casino 71
Castor Bay 35, 37, 42
Central City Library 28, **28**
Cheltenham (Beach) 18, 42, 43
children 43–44
cinemas 72, 73, **73**
Civic Theatre 72, **72**
Clevedon Valley 67
climate 6, 7, 84
clothing 87
clubs 70, 71
Coast to Coast Walk 45–46
Collectors Market 53
Commercial Bay 10
communications 89–90
concerts 72
Cook, James 9
Cornwall Park 29, **29**
Cornwallis Park 33
Cornwallis peninsula 33
Couldrey House 78, **78**
Creative New Zealand 13
cruises 20, 44, 48, 87
cuisine 60, 64
currency 88
customs 85
cycling 49

D
Davies Bay 33
Devonport **7**, 10, 18, **18**, 34, 46
Devonport Wharf 18
Devonport Wine and Food Festival 76
DFS Galleria 50
dolphin watching 44
Domain *see* Auckland Domain
Dove Meyer Robinson Park 10, 31
drinks 65–66

E
East Coast Bays 34–35
Eastern Beach 42
economy 11–12

General Index

Eden Garden 30
Eden Park 43
Edge, The 47
Elam Art School 13, 21
electricity 90
Ellerslie Flower Show 26
emergencies 91
entertainment 70–77
environment 7
Ericsson Stadium 43, 72
etiquette 84
events 74, 75
Ewelme Cottage 31, 38

F
ferries 18, 20, 48, 89
Ferry Building 27
festivals 74, 75–77
film 19, 72
food *see* cuisine
Force Entertainment Centre 47
Frank Sargeson Centre 21
French Bay 33

G
Galbraith Brewing Company 66
galleries *see* museums & galleries
Goat Island Marine Reserve 79
government 11–12
Great Barrier (Island) 54, 82, **82**
Grey, Sir George 83

H
Hauraki Gulf 7, 34, 36–37
Hauraki Gulf Marine Park 37
health 86, 90
Henderson Park 36
Herald Theatre 72, 73
Herne Bay 10

High Street 50
Highwic 38
hiking 44, 48
Hilton Hotel **54**, 55
history 8–11
Hobson Bay 27
Hobson, William 6, **8**, 9
Howick Historical Village *see* museums & galleries
Hunua Ranges Regional Park 25

I
information centres 84–85
Islington Bay 37

J
jazz 77
Jervois Road 32
JF Kennedy Memorial Park 15, 37
Jubilee Building 31

K
Karangahape Road **13**, 32, 51
Karekare (Beach) 19, 42, 43
Kauri Point Centennial Park 35
Kawau 83
kayaking 25
Kelly Tarlton's Antarctic Encounter and Underwater World 17, **17**, 27
Killarney Park 35, 36
Kinder House 31
Kitchener Park 35
kiwi 23, **23**
Kohimarama 43

L
Lake Pupuke 35–36
land 7
language 91
Lantern Festival 76

Le Roys Bush 35
Leigh 79
Ligar Creek 10
literary walks 18, 47
literature 13, 18
Little Barrier 36, 81
Loaded Hog **68**, 69
Logan Campbell, Sir John 10, 29
Long Bay 25, 26, **26**, 35, 42, 43
Lopdell House 33, **33**, 72, 73
Louis Vuitton Cup 15

M
Maidment Theatre 72
Mairangi Bay 35
Mansion House 83, **83**
Mansion House Bay 83
Manukau (Harbour) 6, 25, 33
Manukau City 11
Manurewa Native Bush Reserve 35
Maori 8, 14, 24, 30, 37, 84
Maori Bay 25
Maritime Trail 15
markets 52–53
Marsden, Samuel 9
Mason, Bruce 36
Matakana 79
Mathesons Bay 79
Mathew, Felton 10
Maungakiekie 29
Maungawhau *see* Mount Eden
Mawhitipana Bay 80
McCahon, Colin 40
Mechanics Bay 27
Medlands Beach 82, **82**
Michael Joseph Savage Memorial (Park) 15, 27, 48, **48**
Milford 35, 42, 47
Mission Bay 27, **27**, 42, 43, 48
money *see* currency

General Index

Montana Mission Bay Jazz and Blues Streetfest 76
Motuihe 36
Motutapu Island 37
Mount Cambria Reserve 18
Mount Eden 10, 15, 30, **30**
Mount Eden Domain 30, **30**
Mount Eden village 30
Mount Hobson 82
Mount Victoria 15, 18, **18**
Mount Wellington 15
mountain biking 25
Muriwai (Beach) 19, **19**, 25, 42, 43
Murrays Bay 35
museums & galleries
  Auckland Art Gallery Toi O Tamaki 13, 21, 39–40, **40**
  Auckland Museum 13, 14, **14**, 21
  City Art Gallery 21
  George Fraser Gallery 13, 21
  Howick Historical Village 39
  Museum of Transport and Technology (MOTAT) 22
  New Gallery 13, 39, 40
  New Zealand National Maritime Museum 20, 27
  War Memorial Museum 14
music 72

N
Narrow Neck 42
New Gallery see museums & galleries
New Zealand National Maritime Museum see museums & galleries
Nga Puhi 9
Ngati Whatua 9
nightlife 70–71
North Head **7**, 15, 18
North Shore 9, 11, 34
Northcote 34, 38
Northcote Point 9

O
observatory 29
Okahu Bay 27
Okura estuary 26
Okura Scenic Reserve 26, 35
Old Government House 46
Omaha Flats 79
One Tree Hill 10, 15, 29
Onehunga 45, 46
Oneroa 80
Onetangi 80
opera 72
Orakei Domain 27
Orewa 42
Otahuhu 8
Otara Fleamarket 52–53, **53**

P
Pacific Ocean 6, 8
Pakiri 79
Palm Springs Thermal Pools 44
Papakura 11
Paratai Drive 27
parks 7, 25
Parnell 10, 51
Parnell Road 31, **31**
Parnell Seawater Baths 31, 44
Pasifika Festival 77
Paturoa Bay 33
penguins 17, **17**, 23
people 12, **12**
Philips Aquatic Centre 44
Piha 19, 42, 43
plants 26, 30
Point Erin 9
Point Resolution 15
Ponsonby 10, 32, 51
population 6, 10, 11
Port Fitzroy 82
post offices 89–90
Princes Wharf 27
pubs see bars
Pukekaroa 14
Pump House **35**, 36, 72, 73

Q
Quay Street 27
Queen Street 10, **11**, 50
Queens Wharf 27

R
Rainbow's End Amusement Park 44
Rakino 36
Rangitoto Channel 18, 27, 34, 36
Rangitoto Island 7, **7**, 15, 27, 34, 36, 37, **37**
recreation 25, 41–43
regatta 74, 75
regional parks 25, 44
Remuera 10, 51
Renall Street 32
restaurants 60, 61, 62–64
Robinson, Sir Dove Meyer 10
Rothesay Bay 35
Royal New Zealand Navy 18
rugby 42–43
Russell 9

S
safety 90–91
sailing 15, 20, 41, **41**
seasons 6, 7, 84
Selwyn Domain 48

General Index

Shakespear (Regional Park) 25, **25**
shops **13**, 31, 32, 33, 50–52
Siddell, Peter 12
Sir Keith Park Memorial Site 22
Sky City Casino 71
Sky City Theatre 72
Sky Tower **6**, 16, **16**, 71
Smiths Bush 35
sport 41–43
St Heliers 27, 42, 43
St Mary's Church 31, 39
St Stephen's Chapel 31
Stardome Observatory 29
Starlight Symphony concerts 76
Stony Batter 80
surfing 42
swimming 19, 25, 26, 27, 34, 35, 37, 42, 43
Sylvan Park 35

T
akahe 36, 81
Takapuna (Beach) 34, **34**, **37**, 42, 43, 46
Takapuna (suburb) 34
Takapuna Market 34, 53
Takatu 79
Tamaki Drive 27, 31, 48
Tamaki Isthmus 6, 8, 45
Tamaki Strait 36
Tamaki-makau-rau 8, 11
Tasman Sea 6, 8, 19, 24

Tawharanui Regional Park 79, **79**
Te Henga 19, 42
Te To-waka 8
telephones 89
tennis 43
Tepid Baths 44
theatres 72–73
thermal pools 44
Thorne Bay 35, 36, 47
Three Lamps shopping centre 32
time 89
tipping 60, 88
Tiritiri Matangi (Island) 36, **36**, 81
Titirangi 33
Torbay 11, 35
Torpedo Bay 18
tours 48–49
Town Hall 72
transport 86–87, 88–89
Tryphena 82
tuatara 23, **81**

U
University of Auckland 21, **21**

V
Viaduct Harbour 15, **15**, 20, 27, 45, 46
Victoria Park Market 44, 53
views 15
volcanic cones 7, 15, 16

W
Waiheke (Island) 11, 36, **66**, 80, **80**
Waiheke Jazz Festival 77
Wai-o hua 9

Waitakere (City) 11
Waitakere Ranges 7, 11, 15, 21, **24**
Waitakere Ranges Regional Park 24, 25
Waitakere Tramline Society 24
Waitemata Harbour 6, 9, 10, 15, 18, **18**, 27, 36, 37, 41
Waitemata Waterfront 27, **27**, 31
Waiwera Thermal Resort 44, 78
walks 18, 26, 35, 45–47
Warkworth 79
water taxis 20
Wenderholm (Regional Park) 25, 78
West Wave Aquatic Centre 44
western coast 19, **19**
Western Springs Stadium 72
Westhaven Marina **6**, 41
whale watching 44
Whangaparaoa Peninsula 25, **25**, 36, 81
Whangaparapara 82
Whatipu 19, 33
Windsor Reserve 18
wineries 66, 67, 79
wines 60, 61, **65**, 65–66, 67
Winter Garden 14, 72
Wood Bay 33